AWAKENING

A **40-Day Guide** to Unleashing Your Spiritual Powers, Life's Purpose, and Manifesting Your Dreams!

Rev. Dr. Erin Fall Haskell

ERIN FALL HASKELL INTERNATIONAL, INC.

LOS ANGELES, CA

Published by Erin Fall Haskell International, Inc.
Publisher's Note: This book is not intended for medical advice and does not prescribe
any form of process for the cure or treatment of any emotional, psychological, or
physical ailment directly or indirectly.
The publisher and author assume no responsibility for your personal actions.
This book is for inspirational purposes only.

Speaking and interview inquires contact erin@erinfallhaskell.com

Awakening Series/ 1st ed.
Book Editors: Dr. Karen Lissette Molano & Nicola Victoria Buck
Book Design: Franziska Haase
Jacket photography by Jake Roth

Library of Congress Control Number: 201790954

Hardback ISBN 978-0-9991052-3-8
Paperback ISBN 978-0-9991052-0-7

In dedication to my stillborn son
who gave me the greatest gift of my life: *Awakening.*

Four Steps to Awakening

Step I: Wake Up
Step II: Reprogram
Step III: Align
Step IV: Affirm

Contents

Step IV: AFFIRM

Introduction

It was 4 a.m. on a warm starry summer night when my eyes popped wide open. The first thing I thought was, "I get to go back in!" Excited, I jumped out of bed, threw on my robe, went in my closet, lit the candle, sat down in meditation position, closed my eyes, and began to breathe. Every time I had been going back "in," the veil of life was coming off just a little bit more. Little did I know that tonight would be different. That night in 2006, my entire world changed. Within minutes of sitting in meditation, I heard *The Voice*.

It had been twelve years since I began my spiritual quest; twelve years since I held my stillborn son's body in my arms, realizing he was gone, but his body was still here, knowing that we are not these bodies. In that moment, I committed to my spiritual journey.

For over a decade, I had been meditating, reading every philosophical book under the sun, attending retreats, creating vision boards, and doing my daily spiritual practice, but nothing could prepare me for what was to take place that evening. As I heard *the voice*, I looked around wondering if someone was in my closet with me. As I turned my head to see if anyone was there, the clouds outside the window caught my eye. In a split second, the veil of life came off. I separated from my body, experiencing myself as one with the *Universe*. With a flash of light, I had the greatest epiphany I had ever experienced. My entire identity shifted into one of *Divine*. I began to laugh out loud, as if I had just been told the cosmic joke of the *Universe*. I was free!

After that warm star-filled night in 2006, life became a bit more challenging. I told a few of my close friends what had happened, but they all looked at me as if I were crazy, so I decided to keep my story to myself. As they say, "I stayed in the closet with my spirituality" (No pun intended).

I felt like I was going crazy, but the more I would go back into meditation, the more real the ethereal realm grew, and the less the physical reality became.

So, I stand here today with my heart wide open, vulnerably coming out of the spiritual closet. The journey of my awakening has been the hardest work I have ever done, yet, the most rewarding. Letting go of the cultural programming, belief systems, and the amnesic human state has been intense work, to say the least.

As a Doctor of Divinity, my intention for writing this book is to assist and support people globally in their *Awakening*. This book is not for people who want to manifest a bunch of material belongings or gain spiritual status. Manifesting without *Awakening* is like entering a maze hoping to arrive at some destination, but instead, you keep encountering dead ends. Nothing in the outer world will ever fill the void inside. Material belongings alone will never fulfill the soul's desire of love, connection, and self-expression. This book is for people who are ready to go from being the caterpillar to transforming into the butterfly. It is for the true seekers who desire to know themselves, and in turn, make a difference in the world. And yes… claim their birthright of prosperity!

Awakening can happen over decades, or it can happen like a bolt of lightning. It can be an intense experience, or one of ease, grace, and momentum of downloading the *Universal Truths*. There is usually an integration phase; a shifting from the old identity to the new *Divine* identity. Once you get past this transitional phase (I call it the cocoon phase), you can go back to regular life, being in this world, but not of this world.

WE ARE IN THE GREATEST QUANTUM LEAP KNOWN TO MANKIND; A NEW ERA OF AWAKENING

There is something emerging; it is something you cannot see with the naked eye. It is like a riptide that carries you out to sea into an abyss to the undercurrent that flows below the surface of the ocean, as it takes you beyond the realms of your imagination. At times, it feels scary, as if you are losing control of a ship's sail, navigating through unknown forces and directions. You direct the sail to shore, but the more you resist the current, the further away you are pulled. It is the unexplainable, the indescribable, which leads to the ultimate experience, *Awakening!*

It is the inner conflict, the resistance that pulls you, the desire to break free from the chains of your mind. It is the metamorphosis inside your soul; the transformation within.

There is no need to trek to the Himalayas to find the answers to the *Universe*. *Awakening* is not just for the prophets, or the mystics, or those that have made history. *Awakening* is your birthright, right here, right now.

The truth is that everything you have ever desired to know has always been within you the entire time. When you finally arrive at this knowing, you are home, in the everlasting kingdom of the sacred heart where miracles occur; you are in heaven. You are here to remember the extraordinary nature of who you are!

In this book, you will be guided through four sections, each with its own intention, where all spiritual paths lead to one destination: *Within*. Always remember, there is no right or wrong way, only your way. Follow your path and be true to yourself in the process.

Step I: Wake Up!

It all begins with a powerful decision to *Wake Up*. The first process of *Awakening* is the shift within, changing how you view reality. This transformation starts by understanding how your perceptions set *Universal Law* and the creative process into motion. Noticing how all of life is one serendipitous moment, you will understand the impact of the beliefs within your soul. Discover the grand symphony of the body, mind, and spirit, and how this connection affects your ability to manifest. Embark on learning the difference between universal truths and relative truths, finding your authentic way. Discover how living your *Truth* will set you free.

Step II: Reprogram

Spiritual work is counterintuitive; it is the opposite of learning, because it means letting go of fixed ideas. As you peel back the layers of all you are not, you reveal the *Truth* of who you are. Set forth to clear your *Consciousness* of everything that keeps you from your highest purpose. It is not about figuring it out; it is about allowing something to emerge from within you. This is the time to unburden your soul from all the programming that is holding you back from your success. This section is all about expanding and commanding your *Subconscious* and informing *Universal Law*.

Step III: Align

Allow yourself to flow with life by living your *Truth* and aligning with the *Laws of the Universe* in the four areas of your life.

Wealth and Wisdom: Prepare to lead the journey to empty your *Consciousness* of limiting beliefs about money, wealth, and affluence. Learn how to tap into the infinite innovation within, and embody the wisdom of the *Universe*, which will benefit all aspects of your life. This wisdom will give you the power to claim your birthright of prosperity, abundance, and thriving creativity.

Love and Relationships: Learn to unveil the *Truth* that the ultimate relationship is found within you, and realize that all other relationships are a reflection and projection of your ability or inability to love. Strengthen your aptitude to respond in a positive manner regardless of what occurs in your life and then manifest what your heart truly desires. You will learn about topics such as dating, sex, relationships, communication, and love. Despite the challenges you face, you can transform your relationships from divided to *Divine*.

Health and Wellness: You have an innate power to heal. You have a life force capable of miracles. Let go of your preconceived notions of wellbeing, release negative energy, and uncover the secret to vitality, longevity, and wellness. Discover that the same energy that creates illness, frees you with unlimited potential to manifest wellness. Prepare to discover how health is a conscious choice; a choice that will align with natural laws and Mother Nature.

Purpose and Calling: Unveil the creative spirit within by transforming the most difficult circumstance you have ever endured into the greatest blessing of your life. You will discover new depths through service, expression, and monetization. Multi-dimensional miracles happen. You have a gift to give to this world: YOU!

Step IV: Affirm

This is a journey into the miracle of listening. Create your personal Vision, Life's Purpose Statement, and Daily Spiritual Practice. Whether you are advanced or just a beginner, the miracle of listening is found in the practices of meditation, mindfulness, language, visioning, intuition, affirmative prayer and affirmations, and 40-day practices. Mastering these powerful skills unleashes the voice within so you can think, speak, and create a world surpassing anything you have ever imagined. Through embodying this work, life transcends. Let's embark on this incredible journey together.

How to Use This Book

Awakening is a step-by-step guide divided into 40 chapters to be read one per day. Each chapter has an exercise to assist you in unleashing your spiritual powers, life's purpose, and manifesting your dreams.

I have organized it to take you through the four steps of *Awakening*: deciding to wake up, reprogramming your mind by expanding and commanding your *Subconscious*, aligning with your *Truth* and *Universal Law*, and affirming through your daily spiritual practice.

The last nine days (32-40) are Daily Spiritual Practices. This section is a roadmap for creating your Life's Purpose Statement, and creating your personal Daily Spiritual Practice. It is also a handbook for meditation, mindfulness, language, visioning, intuition, affirmative prayer and affirmations, and 40-day practices. Feel free to go to this section to find answers and begin your spiritual practice along the way.

Step 1:

WAKE UP!

Day 1

Serendipity: Miracles Every Moment

The game of life is a game of boomerangs. Our thoughts, deeds and words return to us sooner or later with astounding accuracy.

~ Florence Scovel Shinn

On June 22, 1998, the Universe rotated 180 degrees. Not in reality, but in a multiverse kind of way. I was watching the classic movie *The Wizard of Oz* late at night, when I had a major epiphany.

This famous movie is about a young girl from Kansas named Dorothy who is swept away in her house by a cyclone with her dog Toto. Her home is dropped on top of the Wicked Witch of the East in the Land of Oz, where she is met by the Good Witch of the North. The witch gives her a pair of red ruby slippers and tells her that the only way for her to return home is for her to visit the Emerald City and ask the Wizard of Oz for help.

Following the yellow brick road, she meets a Scarecrow who wants a brain, a Tin Man who wants a heart, and a Cowardly Lion who wants courage, and invites them to go with her to meet the Wizard of Oz with the hope he can help all of them. After a long stream of events and realizing no one can help them, Glinda, the Good Witch, tells Dorothy, "You've always had the power to go back to Kansas." Then the Scarecrow asked, "Then why didn't you tell her before?" Glinda replies, "Because she wouldn't have believed me. She had to learn it for herself."

Right in front of my eyes, directly from the television screen, came the secret of *Awakening*, summed up in the greatest statement I had ever heard, "You had the power the entire time!"

Chills trickled down my arms. It was the answer I had been seeking; the key to my *Awakening* summed up in one clear statement backed by *one thing* that unlocked that power: *Belief.* The only thing that holds us back from *Awakening* to the power within is our beliefs!

ALL OF LIFE IS DESIGNED FOR YOUR *AWAKENING*

As you go down your own yellow brick road of life, experiencing the good times and the challenging times, realize that every drop of life is designed for your fate: *Awakening*. And, in your *Awakening*, all of life becomes a wonderland of your creation.

Wouldn't it be amazing if you could walk through life having everything you have ever desired show up in a divinely succinct way? What if everywhere you went, miracles and manifestations of your choosing just appeared? What if life was one big serendipitous symphony, reflecting to you your innermost thoughts and desires?

I invite you to consider that you are already there. Yes, everything you are experiencing in this moment is mirroring what is happening within your *Consciousness* in a serendipitous manner.

MIRACLES ARE ONLY GLITCHES IN YOUR CURRENT BELIEF SYSTEM

The word *serendipity* was first coined in 1754 by Horace Walpole to describe a fortunate happenstance, a pleasant surprise, wherein one discovers something seemingly without instigating a search to find it. Today, the *Oxford English Dictionary* (1989) defines serendipity as "the occurrence and development of events by chance in a happy or beneficial way." Serendipity has always been a word synonymous with a positive, joyous response to our surroundings or life experience; a beautiful moment where life feels extraordinary. I am sure you can recall a time when you had the urge to phone a friend just seconds before they call you. Perhaps you have always wanted to live in San Francisco, and then your boss promotes you into your company's San Francisco location. Maybe you meet someone and connect in a way that feels as if you have known that person your entire life. Perhaps you stumble upon a heart-shaped shell as you walk along the beach after asking the *Universe* for a sign to validate your feelings. Serendipitous instances are all around you. We all have experienced them in one way or another. It is the *Universe* giving you a reassuring wink that you are on the right path.

You see, serendipitous moments are not accidents. What if you could harness the power to tap into miraculous discoveries on a regular basis and attract them into your daily life? Wouldn't that be amazing? Over the years, scientists have expressed incredulous awareness that major breakthroughs, discoveries, and inventions have occurred because of serendipitous moments. Had the apple fallen behind Sir Isaac Newton, rather than hitting him on his head, would he still have discovered gravity? Or would we still be mystified, contemplating whether what goes up really comes down? What if biologist, Alexander Fleming, had tidied his laboratory before taking a vacation? Would his staphylococci culture have had the time and atmosphere to grow a fungus that would lead him to discover penicillin? Would humanity have missed out on one of the most important discoveries in medicine? The invention of penicillin, a drug that has saved millions and millions of lives, is a direct result of this so-called *accident* ("ACS, n.d.).

Is a serendipitous instance what leads to innovation, or is it the *observation* of the moment and its psychological process which produces such phenomenon? Psychologist Drew Boyd (2013) poses that what we generally consider serendipitous inventions, can in fact, all be reduced to either a heuristic or an algorithm. If we chart serendipitous moments over time, patterns surface which can be used and codified as innovation on demand. Psychologically, the happy, joyous, rewarding feelings these discoveries bring can be misidentified as serendipitous, when in fact they are not coincidental. Serendipity is a name we have given the phenomenon of *Consciousness*.

If you take the Dalai Lama's (2005) perception of the *Universe* as being one giant living organism like a structure of cells that all exist and operate in relation to one another, then surely you must acknowledge the potential of serendipitous patterns and how they relate to the vibrations you are putting out to the *Universe*. All your cells have their own *Consciousness* and can communicate with each other even when there is distance between them (Backster, 1968).

Information and biological instruction are encoded in every living cell. Organisms grow and advance as these cells divide, reorganize, and replicate, carrying the encoded information and copying it into the new cell. A child can grow and develop because cells are able to replicate themselves, carrying all the encoding information and copying it into the new cell. Deoxyribonucleic acid (DNA) is the molecule that holds these codes, the genetic instructions that tell your cells how to develop and function (The Tech, 2013).

What if this encoded information was present not just in human beings and animals, but in every cell, atom, and particle that makes up the *Universe*? Information is transferred, duplicated, and functions and develops in every morsel of the *Universe*. All you need to do to communicate is listen and respond. Now imagine that these *serendipitous moments* are one way that the *Universe* is communicating with you.

In 2011, NASA confirmed they had located the nucleobases (molecules that carry information), Adenine and Guanine, in pieces of meteorites found in Alaska. The matter, proven to have come from space, contained these two essential building blocks for our very own DNA, telling us that meteorites and rocks impacting our planet were likely to have influenced the creation of life. Moreover, this information supports the notion that all matter is constructed from the same base (Choi, 2011).

Hypoxanthine and xanthine, two chemicals found in muscle tissue and used in biological processes, were also present in these rocks. The cells can communicate and instruct each other to grow when they are in close proximity, as proven by the development of the human body. The *Universe* has also been shown to be constructed from the same chemicals, which tells us that it no longer seems farfetched for us to be able to communicate with the *Universe* (Choi, 2011).

While many consider serendipity to be a magical force outside of our control, it is likely that these same people believe negative events or not-so-lucky occurrences do not follow the same patterns. *Zemblanity*, though not yet formally defined in dictionaries, is the term used to describe when unhappy, unlucky, negative, and expected discoveries are made by design ('Zemblanity, n.d.). This seems easy to accept considering the human psychological need to use patterns to explain experience.

The *Law of Correlation* teaches you that the *Universe* reflects to you exactly what you emanate, as a direct result of your beliefs, thoughts, feelings, and actions. Positive, joyous, and serendipitous instances are not the only moments that give you guidance. Those troublesome situations, those negative instances, are also in place to move you forward. Having awareness of which thoughts and beliefs are keeping you from your full potential, and feeling and understanding when you are in tune with your inner being, will ultimately lead to the all-knowing connection: *Awakening.*

Serendipity and zemblanity are both wake up calls. The *Universe* is constantly nudging you to your *Awakening* and to be the greatest possible version of yourself. Your *Subconscious* is working behind the scenes 24/7, in cahoots with life, scheming up *Divine* plans of perfect reflections of your beliefs. The situations you experience are there to remind you that you are a miraculous being, and to present lessons to assist in your personal development.

The question is, are you ready to tap into your own unique personal power? Are you ready to experience love and serendipity everywhere in your life? Harnessing this ability is simple. Take anything that has happened in your life that you perceive as negative, find a way to see these circumstances as a blessing for you to wake up, and watch your life transform. For example, you might think of a time you lost your job. At the time, you may have considered yourself to be in a very unfortunate situation, but looking back, you can see how this situation has now placed you in a circumstance that is much better than what you ever expected.

It can be difficult to see the positive or galvanizing qualities that painful or difficult experiences provide, but if you focus, you will see how every single experience shaped, molded, and directed your life today. Every drop was created from the very core of your *Consciousness*. Some of you will wonder, "how can losing my job, or suffering a broken relationship or illness be the best thing that ever happened to me? How did I create it?" This is the shift that must take place for your *Awakening*. Once you open your heart with gratitude and acknowledge the painful circumstance as the impetus for your *Awakening*, then you will find a new opportunity to expand.

When you truly believe that the *Universe* is working for your greater good, you will begin to observe how it is all miraculous, guiding you to the grandest version of yourself. You are the creator of your experience. The less you resist what you naturally want to attract, and the more you embrace the circumstances of your life as the opportunity to expand your *Consciousness*, the faster you will experience your *Awakening*.

Day 1 Practice

DECIDE TO WAKE UP

LAW OF PURE POTENTIAL

At the core of you is infinite Consciousness; the connection between your individual Consciousness and your Cosmic Consciousness. There is an unending Divine Source within. All energy is pure potential until it is observed and informed. Your beliefs set the limit of demonstration of principle, which of itself is without limit. It is ready to fill everything because it is infinite. Your ability to have abundance is entirely a question of your own reciprocity to this Universal Intelligence.

Today's practice is to **DECIDE TO WAKE UP!**

On a scale from 1-10 answer the following:
(1= No, not at all & 10 = Yes, completely)

How committed are you to waking up?
1   2   3   4   5   6   7   8   9   10

How much do you believe you have the *power* to create your reality?
1   2   3   4   5   6   7   8   9   10

How much do you believe that you create your financial situation?
1   2   3   4   5   6   7   8   9   10

How much do you believe that you create the relationships in your life?

1 2 3 4 5 6 7 8 9 10

How much do you believe that you create the status of your health?

1 2 3 4 5 6 7 8 9 10

List 3 beautiful things you have created in your life:

1. _____

2. _____

3. _____

I, _____ (your name) have decided to WAKE UP to the *Truth* of who I am and powerfully create a life I love!

Day 2

The Grand Symphony: Body, Mind & Spirit

Life is the whim of several billion cells to be you for a while.

~ Groucho Marx

It was 1994, when the Beatle's song *Yesterday* vibrated through the water of the famous experiement by Masaru Emoto. He decided to freeze water and research how it was affected by occurrences, such as showing letters, pictures, playing music, and by praying to the water. After two months of trial and error, the method bore results showing that positive words, good music, and prayer, produced beautiful crystals. In turn, negative words and discordant music produced opposite results of disfigured crystals (Emoto, 2010).

His book, *The Hidden Messages of Water,* hit the New York Times Bestseller list, breaking the paradigm of what was possible in the realm of the body-mind-spirit connection. Knowing that the human body is made up of 70% water, he was convinced that people were being impacted by the vibration of their thoughts and words.

When we are young, we are taught that our minds, bodies, and spirits are separate entities. In truth, *Mind, Body* and *Spirit* are one. *Spirit* can be defined as non-quantifiable energy that

flows through all living things. Metaphysically, it is the *Consciousness* within a person. *Spirit* is derived from the Latin word *Spiritus,* meaning breath. It breathes life into the mind and body. The body is the physical structure: the bones, flesh, and organs. The mind is the untouchable aspect: *The Conscious Mind*, the *Subconscious* mind, and the *Universal* mind. The link between body and mind is your interpretation of the senses (sight, smell, sound, touch, and feelings). *Spirit* is the captain of the ship. It commands the *Subconscious* mind and the body together as one as we create the beliefs that rule our minds. You are the *Spirit* that is the conductor of the greatest symphony ever created. That's right, you are it!

If you do not develop an intimate relationship with your Higher-Self, *Spirit*, then you will often lack direction in life, finding yourself running around in circles, repeating the same mistakes, and doing the same things over and over expecting a different outcome. The circumstances may change but the theme of the story stays the same, as the *Universe* continues to bring you more of what you do not want. When you lack connection, your actions are often counterproductive or even harmful to others, creating chaos and discord. But when you reach your *Awakening*, listening to your innate, intelligent, all-knowing guidance, you begin to move in accord with your deeper nature. You become capable of dealing with and working through personal hardships, and you are led to inspired action. You are free to follow your bliss.

Once you accept that your body, your thoughts, and your beliefs are all just parts of who you are, the parts that make up

the whole, then you see their collaboration and realize you are the source that creates your beliefs, thoughts, feelings, and your current emotional and physical well-being. You create your reality. Louise Hay (1984) considers how negative beliefs and thought patterns impact your physical body, fostering environments susceptible to illness and disease. She states that your negative emotions directly affect your biochemistry, bathing every cell in the vibration of health or disease, asserting that you hold the ability to heal your body if you recognize and change your limited thought process. The mind and body are one, thus there is no illness that stands alone.

It is common for patients suffering from long term illness to also experience a mood change or depression. We can argue that positive and negative thoughts play a significant role in our health. Consider how increased and prolonged stress can stimulate feelings of anxiety which then manifest both physically and psychologically.

According to Harvard Health Publications, an inciting incident causes neurotransmitters in the amygdala to transfer impulses to the sympathetic nervous system, stimulating bodily responses. Your heart beats faster and your breathing increases. Muscles become tense and the blood flow is diverted from the abdominal organs to the brain. In short, your body reacts to your perception of stress. Therefore, there are links between anxiety and major disorders including insomnia, gastrointestinal disorders, chronic respiratory disorders and heart disease, phobias, PTSD, OCD and panic attacks. (Harvard Health Publications, n.d.). Regardless of the incident, it is your

perception of the incident that triggers the response. You are a powerful, spiritual being commanding responses within the mind and body.

Let's go further and imagine you could rid yourself of illness by influencing your genes. This is not as far-fetched as you might think. Epigenetics is the new science of self-improvement that locates control outside of the DNA structure. It is possible that the external environment can have a direct effect on genes and influence your vulnerability to disease. If cells can be programmed, then they can be deprogrammed. Non-genetic factors cause the organisms' genes to behave or express themselves differently. Danielle Simmons Ph.D. (2008), asserts that the behavior of a person's genes does not solely depend on the gene's DNA sequence. It is also affected by so-called epigenetic factors. Changes in these factors can play a critical role in disease. Genes can be switched on and off to determine which proteins are used.

Dr. Simmons (2008) informs us that cancer was the first human disease to be linked to epigenetics. According to Dr. Simmons, researchers discovered that diseased tissues from participants with colorectal cancer had less DNA methylation than that of the normal tissue of the same participants. Methylated genes are usually turned off; thus, loss of DNA methylation can lead to abnormally high gene activation. In turn, it alters the arrangement of chromatin. Concurrently, too much methylation can undo the work of protective tumor suppressor genes. If external environment affects the genes in each cell, and cells can be re-programmed to affect your body, then you have

the power to heal yourself. You have been a miracle in the making for a very long time.

Let's take a closer look at the intricacy of your physical body. The average body has around 100 billion nerve cells communicating information faster than a lightning bolt. If you laid out all your nerve cells, the cell thread would wrap around the earth almost 2 ½ times, consisting of approximately 90,000 miles in length (Mastin, 2010). It is no wonder that the hows and whys of our creation are so difficult to grasp. The body is made up of about 37 trillion cells, each having their own specific function, informed by genetic coding, influenced by external environmental factors, all backed and designed by *Spirit*. This inborn intelligence has taken roughly 4 billion years to evolve, through the blood, sweat, and tears of all varieties of reproduction, mutation, and replication. The *Universe* has taken approximately 14.2 billion years to unfold. You are a miracle to say the least.

THE BODY IS THE ULTIMATE TOOL FOR SPIRIT TO COMMUNICATE IN THE PHYSICAL REALM

Per some Buddhists, enlightenment is the wisdom of emptiness. It is the phenomenon of feeling free. One could also say enlightenment is a sense of connection with the energy flowing through the body, mind, and spirit. To truly recognize this relationship is to experience *Awakening*. Plato stated that "the part can never be well unless the whole is well."

This dynamic expression of life can do what no computer can; a culmination of such intricate automatic endeavors that blow our minds. No chemist in the world could calculate the complex reactions that the body performs every nanosecond. You have been endowed with an innate healer that has the infinite intelligence of the *Universe*, the ability to restore wellness, and the power to perform miracles. Now, let's tap into the innate healer within. Life is a very dynamic symphony designed to awaken you to your greatness.

Day 2 Practice

EXPAND YOUR THINKING

LAW OF ONENESS

There is One Presence, One Mind, One Spirit and One Life Source which is Divine Love. This law unifies all people, places and things and it is the interconnectedness of all of life; past, present, and future. You are energetically connected to all of life; your individual conscious mind is connected subconsciously to the subjective mind, which is connected to the Collective Consciousness and the Cosmic Consciousness. You are the divine individual and the Universe, co-creating in the most brilliant way.

Today's exercise is to **EXPAND YOUR THINKING**!

On a scale from 1-10 answer the following:
(1= No, not at all & 10 = Yes, completely)

How much do you believe your body has an innate healer within and an intelligence capable of restoring harmony, well-being, and vitality?

1 2 3 4 5 6 7 8 9 10

How much do you believe your thinking is playing into your happiness, health, and success?

1 2 3 4 5 6 7 8 9 10

AWAKENING

How much do you believe your soul is creating your reality?

1 2 3 4 5 6 7 8 9 10

Take a moment today to imagine that all of life is designed for your *Awakening*. Know that every negative circumstance that you encounter in your finances, relationships, health, and creative expression is *Spirit* (your Higher-Self) sending you *Divine* signs that you are off course from living your *Truth*.

> ➤ What signs or negative symptoms are you experiencing within your life?

> ➤ If your soul could talk, what do you think it is saying to you through these *Divine* signs within your body, mind, and *Spirit*?

> ➤ Knowing that within you is *Divinely* inspired action, what do you feel you need to do to get on course to living the life you were designed to live?

Day 3

Consciousness: The Key

Everything you'll ever need to know is within you; the secrets of the Universe are imprinted on the cells of your body.

~Dan Millman

The *Universe* is listening to you right now. No words need be spoken. It listens through energy, vibration, and frequency. It hears your heart, beliefs, and feelings. It communicates with you 24/7, 365 days a year, every second, for all eternity. You are a unique *Divine* individual; you are the creator, the matter, the energy of this magnificent and connected life force.

The *Universe* is taking your order, "What would you like to have? What would you like to experience? Who would you like to be?" But beware, as the *Universe* does not know the future from the past. It does not know the difference between rich or poor, smart or foolish, charismatic or dull. It does not know good from evil, or right from wrong. It is neutral, focused on the here and now, and always responds with a *YES!*

The *Universe* is working 100% of the time. It does not play favorites. It is the same *Divine* nature in every person, and instantaneously works in direct relation to your perspective and actions. This concept, known as *Universal Law*, reflects your vibration, your thoughts, and your beliefs, delivering the points of view you project. Are you attracting scarcity or abundance?

Are you creating fear or love? Do you vibrate signals of chaos or harmony?

The *Universe* can serve your highest purpose. It is the symphony of all symphonies; the most intricate mathematical equation; the teacher of teachers, the paradoxical cosmic comedian; the ultimate mirror that reflects your soul's images, and it is up to you to determine if those images will be blinding or shining.

The *Universe* is a complex network of intelligence. *Consciousness* is the way in which we relate to this intelligence. *Consciousness* is the awareness of your existence, your surroundings, and your thoughts and feelings on an individual and collective level. When you realize that everything is connected, your perception of life shifts from passive to powerful. *Universal Energy* is intelligence and *Consciousness*; it is the life force. The flow of *Universal Energy* is what creates your world, and when obstacles change the flow of energy, chaos ensues. Because YOU are here to master energy, you have the power to create the life you want.

THE EXTENT TO WHICH YOUR CONSCIOUSNESS IS LIMITED OR EXPANDED IS THE EXTENT TO WHICH YOU WILL EXPERIENCE FEELING DIVIDED OR *DIVINE*

The extent to which your *Consciousness* is limited or expanded, is the extent to which you experience isolation or connectedness, restrictiveness or freedom. You are living in unbelievably exciting times. For eons, philosophers have hypothesized that you are the creator of your experience. Today, quantum physics supports this notion. In fifth century B.C., Socrates taught us that the mind is everything; that what you think, you become (Waterfield, 1990). Plato reinforced this notion, declaring that we can change our reality by changing our mind (Jowett, 2005). Every ounce of matter, including every cell in your body, is informed by the vibration of your thoughts.

In modern society, you have been programmed to believe that you are separate and disconnected from the *Universe*. You must find a way to rediscover the *Truth*. You are life energy and an intricate piece to the puzzle. By embracing this phenomenon, you can discover a new sense of reality. It is through your limiting, self-created, and learned beliefs, that you experience yourself to be separate. Expand your *Consciousness* and tap into your own infinite power.

There are endless ways to expand *Consciousness*. Some of the most effective ways include meditation, visualization, mindfulness, intuition, affirmative prayer, yoga, and knowledge of the workings of the *Universe*. When you realize that you are a spiritual being, an infinite innovator, and that you are full of pure potential, you loosen the chains of limitation. As you expand your *Consciousness*, you open the door to universal *Truths*, connecting you to that infinite, intelligent web. This phenomenon can activate natural gifts such as clairvoyance, psychic abilities, intuitive abilities, mental telepathy, extrasensory perception, and much more.

For centuries, we have been aware of the effect our environment has on our mind. Psychiatry, psychoanalysis, and psychotherapy dominated our interpretation and our perceptions of the human experience throughout the nineteenth and twentieth centuries. The concept that the mind can alter our material world has been consistently proven by scientific study. For example, the achievements of innovator Nikola Tesla, world-renowned inventor, electrical and mechanical engineer and physicist, undoubtedly helped the material evolution of humanity. His vision and accomplishments were deeply rooted in his futuristic viewpoint that science goes hand-in-hand with the modern-day concept of spirituality. Tesla firmly believed that when science incorporates non-physical phenomena, the world will make more progress in one decade than it has in all previous centuries combined. He indicated that to understand the true nature of the *Universe*, we must think of it in terms of energy, frequency, and vibration (Seifer, 2001).

Let's take a moment to consider *Consciousness* from a scientific viewpoint. Today, neuroscientists attempt to define *Consciousness* akin to Descartes' notion, "I think, therefore I am," which implies that the mind is separate from the body, validating the interaction with one another through *Consciousness*. Neuroscientists have located what is perceived as an on-and-off switch for the brain. When the claustrum in the brain is stimulated, immediate physical unconsciousness occurs, yet when it is left unstimulated, a person is awake and physically conscious to perceive all surroundings (Smythies, Edelstein, & Ramachandran, 2014).

Scientists also have found that it is the cerebral cortex that provokes physical *Consciousness* even though it has fewer neurons than other parts of the brain. There are currently two scientific theories to aid our understanding of *Consciousness*. The Integrated Information Theory by neurologist Giulio Tononi, asserts that the *Conscious* experience is a direct result of sensory systems and cognitive processes receiving and integrating information, and that this level of *Consciousness* is irreducible, exists in all humans and animals, and can exist in varying degrees (Oizumi, Albantakis, & Tononi, 2014).

The Global Workspace Theory, developed by neurologist Bernard Baars, asserts that a kind of blackboard exists in our brains, where information lands from our experience and perception of our surroundings. According to this theory, moments are written across the brain's blackboard. They are then sent to other, possibly multiple areas of the brain for further processing and interpretation. The process of sending information throughout the brain is what Baars theorizes to be our *Consciousness* (Baars, 2007).

So, what came first, the chicken or the egg? As of today, scientists and spiritualists would say neither; the observer comes before the chicken and the egg. Science and spirituality are merging, both supporting many of the same *Truths*. They both recognize that cause and effect is in the eye of the beholder. Quantum physics proves this idea, demonstrating that when a particle is set into motion, it can take on multiple facets and has various potentials; however, the moment that a particle is observed, it will display a completely different formation. The scientific *Truth* is that the observer does not only affect reality, it creates it, affirming an inherently *Divine* notion. According to famed physicist Albert Einstein (1954, pg. 45-46), "Science without religion is lame, religion without science is blind."

To prove that human *Consciousness* changes space itself, Dr. William A. Tiller conducted an experiment with advanced meditators as his participants. He provided each one of them with an electrical metal device and asked them to imprint these devices with a specific intention, such as raising or lowering the PH of water. The electrical devices were then placed near jars of water. His findings show that the intentions that were imprinted on the devices altered the PH levels of water, showing evidence that mind affects matter. He also observed that all the water in the laboratory exhibited a PH change over time, proving that if you set an intention consistently, your habit of intention will become reality (Tiller & Dibble, 2009). No one could add more weight to this claim than the world-famous Stephen Hawking, who stated, "the whole history of science has been the gradual realization that events do not happen in an arbitrary manner, but that they reflect a certain underlying order, which may or may not have been divinely inspired."

There is undeniably a correlation and direct relationship between human *Consciousness* and material matter. Quantum physics explains that atoms are made up of vortices of energy constantly spinning and vibrating. In its smallest observed form, physical matter is quite simply energy, and somehow, human *Consciousness* is connected to this energy. Something beyond normal human *Consciousness* influences the behavior of energy in those atoms with such strength that their form and structure are altered. If your mind has the capability of altering the reality in front of you, then the key is to learn how to expand your *Consciousness* and practice how to fully realize your connection to everything around you, within you, and the energy flowing through you. That is spirituality.

ENLIGHTENMENT CAN'T BE TAUGHT; IT MUST BE EXPERIENCED

When you expand your *Consciousness*, you are essentially erasing limiting beliefs and programmed cultural concepts from your thinking; broadening your mind from the individual bounded identity to the universal infinite identity. This is a process of moving from the outer world of effect to the inner world of cause. When you eradicate these false perceptions, you free up restricted energy and transcend your thoughts to whole new levels. Universal *Truth*s from your connected *Consciousness* become your new reality. At this level of *Consciousness*, you feel being one with the *Universe*, experiencing your *Divinity*. You begin not only to understand the potential of free will, allowing yourself to fully play in this physical realm, but you also begin to embody it through co-creating with the *Universe*. This is the process of *Awakening*.

When it comes to *Consciousness*, there is a spectrum between the experience of feeling divided and the experience of feeling *Divine*. In fact, every single person has a unique use of *Consciousness*. You condense and filter the *One Mind* through the individual soul, leaving you with a relative experience. This spectrum is in perfect proportion to your limited beliefs, perspectives, and ways of responding to your environment. To be enlightened means to be one with the knowing of the entire *Universe*. An *Awakening* can be a slow process, as you gradually become more aware of your surroundings, or it can strike you like a bolt of lightning. As you expand your *Consciousness* within your body, your stress levels go down, your blood pressure decreases, your muscles relax, your heartbeat regulates, and your blood sugar levels stabilize. *Consciousness* directly affects your health and well-being. So how do you begin to expand your *Consciousness*? Let's begin with some fun practices.

Day 3 Practice

SEE LIFE AS A MIRROR

THE LAW OF CREATION

Life is being created from Spirit (your Higher-Self) right now. This axiom is the first cause and mode of operation of how the creative process of the Universe works; it is the unfoldment of thought, through Universal Law, into form. This law is based upon the primary axiom of spirituality, the reality that life is created from Spirit (your Higher-Self). Spirit manifests itself in and through all creation, but is not absorbed by its creations. The manifest Universe is the body of Spirit. This creative principle works for everyone equally.

Today's practice is to begin to **SEE LIFE AS A MIRROR!**

➢ Begin to observe the possibility that all of life is the out-picturing and the co-incidence of your *Individual Consciousness*, *Collective Consciousness*, and *Cosmic Consciousness*.

➢ Focus on three things today and see the miracle of each experience; whether it is a lesson or a blessing.

➢ Begin to co-create with the *Universe*, and have fun playing this *Divine* game called life.

Day 4

Manifesting: Co-Creating with the Universe

The true use of thought is that of an instrument of power.

~ Malinda Cramer, Founder of Divine Science

In Menlo Park, New Jersey, on October 22, 1879, Thomas Edison figured out how to direct the same energy that could kill someone into an avenue that would light a light bulb. After trying 6,000 different filaments, he and his team had success.

The light bulb was considered the "Crown Triumph" of Thomas Edison's 1,093 patents. His inventions included the carbon microphone and motion picture camera, the mimeograph and the phonograph, the kinetoscope and stock ticker, and many more. In my opinion, what made him able to manifest so many inventions, was his ability to innovate, collaborate, and use *Universal Energy* for good.

YOU ARE THE *DIVINE INDIVIDUAL* AND YOU ARE THE ENTIRE *UNIVERSE*

The *Universe* is an extension of you, just as you are an extension of the *Universe*. In this interconnected and infinite loop, as you respond to the thoughts and feelings of others and react to your surroundings, the *Universe* responds to you. One of the foundational universal axioms is that you are a spiritual being in a spiritual *Universe* with a *Law of Cause and Effect*. You are endowed with access to everlasting universal energy, and therefore, the same energy that binds you can set you free. To experience freedom, you must learn how to direct the energy towards harmony rather than discord.

You may consider that one of the primary reasons you are here in the physical realm is to actualize the use of your *Consciousness* through the demonstrations you have created and continue to create. Mastering the creative process is the key to *Awakening*. From a universal perspective, you are exactly where you need to be.

If we are going to create a world where we are all thriving, we will have to use *Consciousness* for good. According to Thomas Troward, "Getting things into a better order is the great secret of progress, and we are now able to fly through the air, not because the law of nature has altered, but because we have learned how to arrange things in the right order to produce this result. Consequently, it follows that the first principle of this power must be harmony."

YOU ARE MANIFESTING 24/7 WITHOUT ANY EFFORT WHATSOEVER

One of the greatest misconceptions surrounding manifesting is that you must constantly be *doing* something to create tangible demonstrations; however, everything you perceive creates a vibration of energy that is read, understood, and responded to by *Universal Law* regardless of any action. Your reality is constantly being created by these vibrations that you are consciously and unconsciously emitting to the *Universe*. Remember, the *Universe* does not distinguish; it does not know the difference between past, present, or future, as it is always responding to your current experience and delivering more of the same. You do not need to do anything to manifest; you are manifesting at all points in time. Nonetheless, to manifest what you specifically desire, you must understand the creative process and learn how to co-create with the *Universe*.

What Is a Manifestation?

The entire *Universe* is pure intelligence and endless potential, ready for infinite creation. It is an abundant energy field directed by *Consciousness* through the subjective creative medium, *Universal Law*, into form. Manifestation is the individual use of energy filtered through the limited beliefs induced within the soul, and directed by selection and initiation to create circumstances, objects, relationships, and form. It is the mental equivalent of the individual *Consciousness,* along with the *Collective* and *Cosmic Consciousness*. If you look around, you will see objects that were first imagined, and then manifested into form through innovation, collaboration, and creativity. Consider your body and all the trillions of chemical reactions taking place without a single thought. This is the automated system of the *Subconscious* mind that is linked into the subjective mind, and regulated by *Universal Law*.

Take a step back and start to observe the circumstances of your life: your relationships, your health, your financial situation, etc. These situations are manifestations that you have created through guidance of your *Individual Consciousness*, *Collective Consciousness*, and *Cosmic Consciousness*. You can observe where in life you have chosen to live in alignment with the natural laws, or have chosen to live in discordance. Take another leap back and begin to observe your culture, your political system, and humanity at large. This is the *Collective Consciousness* and *Race Consciousness* that is held within the *One Mind* that is reflected into our current world events. Now let us look back and look at life, Mother Earth, and the *Universe*. They have been created by the same life force that lives within you, only now, all these grand things already created are held in the *Cosmic Consciousness* and no longer need to be tended by the *Individual Consciousness*. Manifestation is the directing of energy through the creative process into form. From an individual perspective, your *Consciousness* may not be expanded enough to supersede the *Collective* or the *Cosmic*, but you always have the choice to experience your personal life according to your perception, initiation, and selection.

You may ask, "Why do I even need to manifest?" Everything you see is a manifestation. As a spiritual being, you are already whole and complete, but from a relative perspective, you are here to experience the depths of your soul in form. If form were not available in an organized physical dimension, substances would be perpetually colliding into one another, there would be no individual expression, and life would always be utter chaos. You chose to come to this Earth to have this experience as a human being. Manifestation is a multi-dimensional game of *Consciousness*. The extent to which you expand your *Consciousness* is the extent to which you experience co-creating with the *Universe*.

How Do I Manifest My Desires?

Every creation begins with *Spirit*, which is the part of you that creates from nothing, the pure *Consciousness* that resides within you. The creative process of manifesting begins with beliefs, which inform *Universal Law*, and manifest into form. Everything is created from spirit-to-mind-to-body and spirit-to-soul-to-form. This is the triune nature of life; every "*thing*" begins with *Consciousness*. The moment you have a consideration, is the moment you set the law into motion. Knowing this, you must learn not only to direct your thoughts, but to consciously and systematically direct your mind. You inform *Universal Law* through the vibration and frequency of the feelings behind your thoughts and in turn, the *Universe* responds through the *Law of Correlation*. In other words, it does not matter what you say or do in life; what matters is what you truly believe within your solar plexus, also known as your *"heart chakra."* Your feelings are what inform the *Universe* what to reflect to you. The secret of all power is your individual ability to direct the *Universal Law of Cause and Effect* through the embodiment of vibration; aligning your *Subconscious* with *Universal Consciousness*. Throughout this book, you will learn how to expand your *Consciousness* and have a greater ability to direct your manifestations to match your desires. The more you practice and focus, the better you will become at having control over your manifestations.

THE EXTENT TO WHICH YOU AWAKEN IS THE EXTENT TO WHICH YOU WILL EXPERIENCE BEING POWERFUL

As you uncover the *Truth*, piece by piece, you begin to release all limited beliefs which keep you from manifesting your true desires. You must learn to use your *Individual Consciousness* to direct energy upon *Universal Law* with a specific intention. You can master this phenomenon through meditation, intuitive practices, *Subconscious* work, affirmative prayer, yoga, and Chakra work, to say the least. The extent to which you expand your *Consciousness* and free it of its limitations is the extent to which you embody the *Universal Truths*. The journey you take is up to your choosing, as all roads will lead to the revelation of the *Truth* within. All growth and manifestation is the result of the embodiment of *Consciousness*. The highest *Consciousness* not only reveals the *Truth*, it reveals the real you!

What Can I Manifest?

The creative medium, *Universal Law*, does not care what you create; it is impersonal. It is an intricate system that simply responds with a "Yes!" It does not play favorites, it does not judge, it just simply reacts to your vibrations. It does not know the difference between manifesting a penny or a billion dollars. It does not know the future from the past, as it just knows the here and now. *Spirit* and the *Heart* are not neutral. Their primary drives are joy, love, connection, and self-expression; therefore, when you are not in alignment, you end up isolating yourself more and more. You are such a good *Spirit*, that when you do not use your energy for harmony, you take your own powers away. Take addictions, for example. If a person's energy creates toxicity and self-indulgence, that person will end up bound. The key to manifestation is to use your energy for the highest good. There are no limits to what you can manifest!

Why Can't I Manifest the Things I Want and Why Does It Take So Long?

Most people live in the objective world, rearranging the circumstances and effects of their lives. They do not realize that life is a mirror of their *Consciousness*. *Universal Law of Cause and Effect* dictates that every action has a reaction and consequence. Your physical reality is a playground where you can experience your own *Consciousness*. This is an extraordinary construct that not only allows you to demonstrate harmony, productivity and love, and allows your hopes and dreams to be fully realized; it also leads you to create bonds, repetitious vicious cycles, entanglement, and chaos. There is no great mystery to manifestation. What is in your *Consciousness* determines what you manifest. Your life is the mental equivalent of the *Individual Consciousness, Collective Consciousness, and Cosmic Consciousness.*

You may be playing devil's advocate thinking, "So does the baby that is born to a meth-addicted mother choose this life?" "What about the Holocaust victims? Did they choose to be in those horrific situations?" You must be reminded of the *Truth* that we are *One*. Those situations are the out-picturing and manifestations of the discord of the *Collective Consciousness* of the world. From a soul level and an individual level, the people that are part of such circumstances have chosen to have an intense relative experience and have great callings to help the world at large. Experience, conditions, physical objects, and the environment, are the culmination of everything that has ever been created from the Collective *Consciousness*.

Criminal and global political breakdowns and wars are the manifestation of our society as an organism. As Mahatma Gandhi is quoted as saying, "be the change you want to see in the world." The extent to which your *Consciousness* is in a state of confusion is the extent to which you will have trouble manifesting your desires. If you want to see peace in the world, you must begin by creating peace within.

The *Conscious Mind* directs the *Outer World*; it is the objective mind that possesses choice, volition, reasoning, and will. It perceives through the five senses and it is capable of inductive and deductive reasoning. The most powerful aspect of the

Conscious Mind is its ability to impress the *Subconscious Mind*. If you want to manifest your dreams, you must learn to command the *Subconscious*, turning habits into automatic actions, and focused thinking into the norm.

The *Subconscious Mind* addresses the *Inner World*, and is linked as one with the *Subjective Mind* and *Universal Mind*. It is this amazing automatic system that takes care of all biological functions and vital processes without sleeping or resting. We do not have to think for our hearts to beat; it is done via the *Subconscious Mind*. This perfect automated system is first directed by the *Conscious Mind*. This incredible system is the storehouse of all memory, and it simply responds via deductive reasoning and performs habits for survival.

The extent to which you direct your *Subconscious* to be in accordance with what you desire to manifest will always match the extent to which you experience living in grace. For example, if your desire is to manifest being the best dancer, you must inform your *Subconscious* with rudimental muscle memory, making dancing effortless. Another example would be a person who desires to be wealthy. This individual would need to inform his or her *Subconscious* into embodying a wealthy mindset. Every manifestation is the direct result of your being. This is the *Law of Attraction*, which begins with *Conscious* thinking that turns into habitual action.

While you are manifesting in this instance, there are things that you wish to manifest that cannot happen overnight as governed by the *Law of Growth*. For example, if you desire to be a ballet dancer, or an astronaut, you must first believe it is possible for you to do this in this lifetime. Then you must tune yourself to the opportunities the *Universe* presents to you that allow you to harness the skills to become what you wish, apply yourself, and physically embody the tenants of each desire. Nothing is impossible. You are the creator of your world experience; however, doubts, negative thoughts and feelings, limited beliefs, and the inability to trust, let go, and believe that the *Universe* will answer your every request, delay you from getting what you want. In turn, you get more of what you do not want.

The societal constructs and illusions mankind has created for itself are what hinder and prevent you from fully knowing your own power, expansion, and potential. How many incidents from your childhood have you carried into adulthood and incorporated into your everyday beliefs? Maybe someone told you that you were good at mathematics, or a bad speller, or a graceful dancer. Good or bad, you habitually classify people and put them into boxes. Some people struggle their whole lives trying to climb out of one of those boxes. What I want you to embrace is the concept that there are no boxes. Your potential, choices, and experiences are limitless. The only person who can keep you imprisoned in any box is yourself. You hold the key to free your entrapped soul. It is clarity, focus, and intention of your personal *Truth* that guides you to expansion, allowing, and receiving. You are a master of energy, so one of the primary disciplines to manifesting your dreams is clarity. Clarity is power. Becoming clear about what you want to manifest can be the most challenging work. You primarily find clarity by emptying your *Consciousness* of everything that is not in alignment with your bliss. Your work is to simply release anything that no longer serves your highest vision. Remember, the *Universe* simply responds. When you focus on what you do not want the *Universe* has to bring you what you do not want. Make a conscious effort and focus on what you do want, even if you do not yet see it. Then release, let go, and believe that it is yours for the taking. Watch your desires manifest into reality, knowing that the work is done. Take a moment to reflect on what you have learned, and expand your *Consciousness*.

Day 4 Practice

TAKE 100% RESPONSIBILITY

LAW OF MANIFESTATION

There are two primary principles of this law: One is Spirit (your Higher-Self), which creates from nothing and in harmony with the unity of life. Through your beliefs within your subconscious mind and soul, you set into motion this Universal Law. The second relates to the degree to which your beliefs are limited and not in accordance with life harmony. This is the degree to which you will experience yourself unable to manifest. Furthermore, serving the highest good exponentially increases your ability to manifest.

Today's practice is to **TAKE 100% RESPONSIBILITY!**

Take ten minutes to contemplate these questions:

➢ What if you took full responsibility for bringing happiness, harmony, peace, and joy to your life?

➢ What would it look like to take on the ability to positively impact everyone and every situation you encountered today?

➢ Where in your life do you experience discord, dysfunction, or disorganization? How could you bring stability and harmony to these situations?

Taking responsibility does not mean you control or force anything. Rather, it means to take inspired action. Anywhere there is strife your goal is to live in faith and cast the burden to *Spirit* so that you can focus on love, joy, and abundance.

To live in positive alignment with *Universal Law* is to release the focus of what you do not want and take responsibility for what you do want.

Faith is essential in taking 100% responsibility because you are an infinite *Spirit* capable of miracles.

Day 5

Transformation: Shift Happens

We do not need magic to change the world, we carry all the power we need inside ourselves already: we have the power to imagine.

~J.K. Rowling

The metamorphosis of the caterpillar to the butterfly is the most classical analogy of transformation. First, the larvae eggs hatch and out crawls the eager, oscillating furry caterpillar, considerably bigger than the larvae egg, excited to crawl its way by land or plant to those luscious leaves, where it can munch and eat to its heart's content. Once the caterpillar has packed itself full of food, it locates the perfect leaf, but instead of crawling across it, it creates a new reality and hangs itself upside down. It begins to create a cocoon or chrysalis, encasing itself in a fine thread where its next metamorphosis takes place. Ten to fourteen days later, the caterpillar re-absorbs its skin and fur, and slowly develops into a beautiful butterfly. When it is ready, the butterfly swallows air to expand its body and breaks open the chrysalis and wraps its legs around the leaf. With its wings, still moist from the protective environment of the chrysalis, the butterfly needs to wait until they are completely dry. Then when it is ready, it spreads its glorious wings, leaves the known dimension of the plant, and takes flight into a new reality, flying and experiencing life and the world in a completely unique way. It is a beautiful cycle that ends where it began; with the adult butterfly laying eggs, ready for new life to spring forth.

The most profound aspect of the butterfly's transformation is that it is born as a caterpillar with what is called imaginal cells and discs, which hold the dormant information for the butterfly's destiny. You too hold within you the consciousness of your destiny, your *Awakening.* Only it is up to you to *decide* to *Wake Up*!

AWAKENING IS NOT ONLY AN EXPANSION OF CONSCIOUSNESS; IT IS AN IDENTITY SHIFT

Spirituality is the reality that everything comes from *Spirit*, your Higher-Self. It is the idea of being the cause rather than the effect of life. It is the paradigm shift from defining yourself through observation of the material world to recognizing the absolute *Truth* of your spiritual nature. It is a victory within—the understanding that all is created from *Spirit*—that *Universal Energy* is flowing through you, as you, connecting you to the entire *Universe*. Though at times, it may feel as if you are swimming against the current of the societal structures we have built and learned; it is your spiritual evolution to seek the *Truth* and be set free!

Transformation is the X factor; the quantum leap of the self, contemplating the self. Just like a math problem, when you change the x in an equation, the entire equation changes along with the results. Thomas Troward (2008) referred to this phenomenon as the *Original Power*. It is in self-contemplation that you instantaneously inform *Universal Law*, setting the *Law of Correlation* into motion. The moment you change your perception of the *Self*, you set polarity into motion, attracting and repelling circumstances, people, and experiences instantaneously.

Change occurs instantly when your perception of yourself changes. There is, and has only ever been, one barrier holding you back from all your dreams and desires, and that is your limited *Consciousness*. Now is the time to make bold choices and declare your own personal revolution.

Most people believe that if they just get enough information, then logic will wrestle its way through and they will instantaneously know what to do and how to change their lives. Or better yet, if they just find enough inspiration, they will be motivated to act. They try to fix, change, alter, manage, adjust, reconstruct, and manipulate unwanted situations to solve problems. This approach never works. You need to address your *Consciousness* to experience transformation. The first process of all spiritual work is to decide; to choose to *Awaken* and to release core beliefs that keep you from reaching your full potential. Do not underestimate the power of a decision. Your life becomes what you have decided it will become.

Let's consider how past decisions have affected and created your current life experience. For many of you, there were moments in your lives which you perceived to be highly traumatic. To survive that traumatic event, you made a decision that altered your way of thinking to be able to cope with the emotional pain. These new beliefs helped you to survive emotional pain, but also prevent you from moving forward.

For example, when children witness their parent's divorce whereby a parent leaves, the child can be left feeling abandoned and very sad. In that moment of trauma, the child may decide to interpret that situation and conclude that people you love will leave. This single incident, backed by poignant feelings, can embed into the *Subconscious*, informing the subjective mind, which in turn, informs *Universal Law,* which brings you more of the same.

This explains why you will witness people creating the same situations repeatedly, reaffirming the observation for the rest of their lives, and preventing them from fully connecting in other relationships. Decisions at a soul level can connect or enforce boundaries of division. These decisions alter your life. You may intuitively know some of the decisions and judgments made in childhood are incorrect, yet you believe them subconsciously, and create the ultimate resistance on your path to happiness. Your shadow counterparts incarcerate you in such a way that you may think more negatively, feel more negatively, and perceive yourself to be less worthy. In turn, your infinite possibilities, potential, and hope, become significantly reduced and diminished.

The *shift* we refer to is a shift in perception of experience. It is the transformation in your reality that embraces the concept that everything comes into fruition from *Spirit*, and it is the recognition that you are the cause, and not the effect of life; a reflection and projection of what is happening within your *Consciousness*. The spiritual shift can happen instantaneously or over time. It can feel like the scariest or the most joyous experience you have ever encountered. It is unique for everyone. It is the greatest journey you will ever take—the union of you and your Higher-Self. This shift could even be galvanized by a physical or mental breakdown, but also has the potential to be the greatest blessing of your life.

BREAKDOWNS ARE CREATED FROM THE DEPTHS OF YOUR SOUL FOR A BREAKTHROUGH IN YOUR *AWAKENING*

There is such beauty in the breakdown. Such perfection. It is the bustling arena where your soul and *Spirit* conspire to demand a new reality to transpire. Knowing this, you will no longer view breakdowns as negative, but better still, as opportunities. They are perfectly *Divine* portals to hatch the butterfly within.

The metamorphosis of the butterfly demonstrates this so beautifully. It goes through such a visually striking transformation that, if we did not have tangible evidence, it would sound like the grandest fairytale ever told.

Similarly, in your human experience, when there is a breakdown in the body or in the mind, it can originate from those early decisions that formed your limited beliefs that something is, should be, or is going to be a certain way. You need to be honest with yourself and register where you are exactly on your personal scale of limited beliefs and work on releasing what holds you back. Do you believe you are worthy of health and high energy? Do you believe food is to nourish you or to temporarily entertain you? Do you believe that you are the cause or the effect of your body? When you realize you are not a prisoner to your beliefs, but rather the creator of them, you can make new choices. Consider that all dis-ease begins within the *Soul.*

Contemplate for a moment that when the body has a breakdown, an interruption of its healthy flow, such as an illness, disease, hormonal imbalance, weight issue, or chronic fatigue, the breakdown could in fact be the soul communicating to you that something is out of balance. This is one way the *Spirit* can be acknowledged and heard.

The Spontaneous Remission Project is a database created by Caryle Hirshberg and Brendan O'Regan (1993) which includes 3,500 references to approximately 800 journals in 20 languages documenting unexplainable Spontaneous Disease Remission. Confirmed cases included instances in which cancer had ceased and disappeared, aneurisms had disintegrated, and HIV positive patients were later found to be HIV negative. Rankin's work outlines how we have the power to instruct our cells to heal and outlines the best environment for cells to be healthy based on an observation of the power of thought.

Keep faith that the *Universe* and all its infinite wisdom, tightly wound in every living cell, is consistently and forcefully working for your evolution. This thought drastically alters any unnerving viewpoint on chaos or upset. Finally, you can see beauty in the breakdown. You witness the shift which your *Spirit* demands so that you can be propelled into the next realm of reality. It is the storm that commands the roots of the tree to grow deeper, thus stabilizing it. The infrastructure of a tree reveals that roots, beneath ground level, often expand 9 meters (30 ft.) beyond the tips of the branches. According to Thomas Perry (1978), the reach of these roots can form a circle with a diameter two or more times the height of the tree. What is visible and experienced in one reality can be connected to another. Sometimes you know there is more to what the eye can see; sometimes you have to look for it, and sometimes you just have to trust that your own expansion, the *Spirit* inside us all, will lead you wherever you need to go, the best way it knows how.

Your *Truth* deepens as you weather each passing storm, allowing you to be enveloped by the ebb and flow of the entire *Universe*, knowing that you are all of it. Transformation is a shift in identity from the individual I to the great *I AM*. It is a shift in *Consciousness*; a realization of the true self.

Day 5 Practice

SHIFT YOUR THINKING

LAW OF CAUSE AND EFFECT

For every effect there is a cause, Spirit (Your Higher-Self). Your beliefs create your thoughts, which create your feelings and emotions, which cause the circumstances of your life. This is the triune nature of the creative process; the unfoldment of thought, through law into form. This law responds in direct proportion to your beliefs. Your experience of life changes to the degree you change your core beliefs and thinking.

Today's practice is to **SHIFT YOUR THINKING!**

For most people, their *Subconscious* has been negatively programmed through the commands they have given it during traumatic experiences. For example, through the trauma of parents getting divorced, a child may program the *Subconscious* to believe "I am not worthy of love," or "Love doesn't last."

➢ What decisions did you make about life, people, and yourself during traumatic incidents?

➢ What commands did you program into your *Subconscious* during emotional states?

➢ How are those limiting beliefs affecting your current life today?

Take 10 minutes to contemplate how the hardest things you have been through could be blessings in disguise. For example, when I had a stillborn son, I also had the epiphany that his body was tangibly present, but he was not. I realized he was a spiritual being and not his body. In that moment, I also realized that I was a spiritual being. The *Universe* is masterful at *Awakening* us to the *Truth*, which is eternal, ever-evolving love.

Day 6

Truth: Live Your Truth!

Only do what your heart tells you.

~Princess Diana

It was another movie night. I curled up on my sofa with a bowl of popcorn and turned on the hit movie *Sliding Doors*. It is a romantic drama about parallel universes, where Helen, the main character, gets fired from her public relations job and discovers her boyfriend is cheating on her. In one universe, after getting fired, she catches the train and arrives home just in time to walk in on her boyfriend in bed with his ex-girlfriend. In the other universe, after getting fired, she first drops her earring in an elevator and then runs to the train, missing it by seconds. She ends up arriving home later, but never catches her boyfriend with his ex-girlfriend. After a long stream of events within the movie, both story lines finish with the exact same ending: she breaks up with her cheating boyfriend and finds herself in a fatefully serendipitous relationship.

In the climax scene, James, her newfound love, is frantically searching for her because she thinks he has cheated on her as well. When he finally finds her, she is on a bridge at night in the rain. He professes that he is not cheating on her. With her hair soaking wet and tears in her eyes, Helen dramatically asks, "Is that the truth James?"

It was as if the Universe was speaking directly to me again, telling me another secret to *Awakening*, summed up in the greatest question ever asked: "Is that the truth?!"

So, what is truth? *The Oxford Dictionary* (1989) defines *Truth* as that which is in accordance with fact or reality; a fact or belief which is accepted to be true or a verified or indisputable fact. There are relative and ultimate truths. Your *Truth* is based on one thing: *Beliefs!*

The Greeks were the first to develop the concept that every person has an individual *Truth*. They were the first to recognize that spirituality is an individual journey. This has been the foundation for many great thinkers and grand inventions. You witness this ultimate *Truth* within the macrocosm as well as the microcosm. You have witnessed an event only to discover that another person experiencing the same scenario had a vastly unique experience and a completely different interpretation of it. You have had domestic disputes with your partners, each struggling to see the other person's view. Science has proven that your sense of reality and perceptions are alterable as witnessed in the *Observer Effect*. This *Effect* proves that observing an act can astonishingly make changes to the phenomenon being observed; the instrument measuring an act influences the state of that which is being observed (Science News, 1998). Similarly, the Hawthorne effect is based on human as opposed to cellular behavior and confirms a form of reactivity in which subjects modify an aspect of their behavior in response to the understanding, awareness, and acknowledgement that they are being observed (Shuttleworth, 2009). Understanding cause and effect, both relative and *Universal Truth*s are essential to finding and emanating your unique relative *Truth*.

Universal Truths vs. Relative Truths

Universal Truths are changeless, eternal, and absolute. They relate to the whole of mankind and our world. The physics of matter such as gravity and *The Law of Attraction* are *Universal Truths*. They are independent of personal interpretation or reflection on it. These underlying core *Truth*s are how energy flows to you, through you, and around you in every living vibrating organism. They are the mechanics of the creative process, regardless of your own individuality. Quite simply, it these laws describe how things work, change, grow, and develop. It is the Universal ebb and flow of existence.

Relative *Truth*s, conversely, are different for every single human being in existence. Einstein's Theory of Relativity is the best way to tackle this concept. Relative *Truth*s are the experimental and metaphysical aspects of life, projected and reflected from your *Consciousness*. Relative *Truth*s are relative to a frame of reference such as language or culture, allowing for your unique interpretation of something according to the values you attribute to an object, experience, or being. They are relative *Truth*s because they are *Truth*s determined by your own perception. One person may find something mind-blowingly beautiful, yet another, may find the exact same thing outrageously ugly, while someone else may find it hilarious. There is no right or wrong response. The interpretation is a relative *Truth* unique to everyone. The experience or object can be the same, but the response may be vastly different from those experiencing it.

When you understand the difference between absolute *Truth*s and relative *Truth*s, you can have and acknowledge opinions and viewpoints without stating them as absolute *Truth*s. Everyone gets to have opinions with the option to evolve and shift these experiential viewpoints. The beautiful concept behind people having differences is that when you come across disagreements with another person, you get the opportunity to understand how they experience life. There is beauty in our differences.

MAY LIVING YOUR TRUTH SET YOU FREE

In my opinion (which is a relative *Truth*), one of the primary points of spiritual work is to birth your unique *Truth*. Maieutics was a Greek Oracle process based on the word "midwifery" because it was a modality of birthing one's *Truth*. Socrates applied this technique to what is now called the Socratic Method. Modern day cognitive therapy applies some of these same tactics within their practice, as do many spiritual healers. Everyone has a unique and *Divine Truth*. It is the *Awakening* through the *Divine* Individual.

One of the keys to *Awakening* is to boldly live your personal *Truth* and allow others to live theirs. When you finally unveil your unique *Divine Truth*, you are set free to express yourself profoundly, unapologetically, and confidently, with beauty and grace. May living your *Truth* set you free. Embrace all that you are and all that everyone else is. We are all parts of the whole, but this life journey is even more wonderful because of our relative *Truth*s; our own and those of others. The beauty is in the differences.

An Ancient Cherokee Tale of Two Wolves

Cherokee legend has it, on a cold November eve, out in the American wilderness and warmed only by the glowing embers of the remnants of a fire long put to sleep, a wizened American Indian Grandfather huddled with his grandson, listening to the sound of the trees. A wolf howled through the darkness summoning its pack to adventure. Fear and confusion etched itself across the young boy's face as he looked to his grandfather for reassurance. His eyes surveyed their surroundings, desperate for affirmation as to where the wolves were. The grandfather studied his grandson, knowing that the wolves were far away. Seeing the opportunity to plant wisdom within the young mind, he placed a firm grip on his grandson's shoulder and bade him to listen. "Be not afraid my child, for there is a battle in each and every one of us; a battle between the fiercest and oldest of wolves. One embodies the darkest smoke of evil, shrouded with anger, envy, jealousy, sorrow, regret, greed, arrogance, self-pity, guilt, resentment, inferiority, lies, false pride, superiority, and ego. The other is good. It is joy, peace, love, hope, serenity, humility, kindness, benevolence, empathy, generosity, *Truth*, compassion, and faith. These wolves have faced each other and boldly stood their ground since time began. The grandson softened, listened to the old man, comforted by his warmth and touch. He turned to face his grandfather and gently shuddering asked, "Which wolf wins?" Moonlight shimmered across the old Cherokee's face "The one you choose to feed."

Awakening begins with getting in touch with your personal relative *Truth* and the *Universal Truths* of the *Universe*. We all have that voice within that desires to take us down the road of negative thinking. We all must win the battle within and live a life that is in alignment with *Universal Truths*.

Day 6 Practice

ACCEPT PEOPLE'S VIEWPOINTS

LAW OF RELATIVITY

What occurs on a microcosm level is what happens on the macrocosm level. Spiritual Truth and Universal Laws are absolute Truth; however, they can be individually used for a relative perspective and experience. People are endowed with the individual use of the One Mind in the exact portion and distortion they choose at a soul level. Furthermore, your individual reality is in direct relation to the whole.

Today's practice is to **ACCEPT PEOPLE'S VIEWPOINTS!**

One of the highest spiritual abilities is to accept people as they are, allowing others to have their own personal *Truth*. Today's exercise is to:

- ➤ Practice non-judgments and non-resistance.
- ➤ Allow others to have their own relative viewpoints about life.
- ➤ Simply become fascinated by how people choose to perceive their circumstances and the world.
- ➤ Release the need to have others have the same viewpoint as you.
- ➤ Allow others to be who they are.
- ➤ Know that each person's path is unfolding perfectly.

The *Truth* is they are *Divine* spiritual beings with the power to create anything they choose!

Step 2:

REPROGRAM

Day 7

Emptying Your Cup and Releasing Fear

Empty your cup so that it may be filled; become devoid to gain totality.

~Bruce Lee

A scholar, deemed an expert in Nirvana Sutra, proud of his extensive background in Buddhism, approached the Great Master. He eagerly performed the customary bows and asked him to teach him Zen. Before the Zen Master could utter a word on his request, the Buddhist Scholar launched into a long speech outlining his impressive achievements, all the multitudinous doctrines and sutras he had studied, and the vast knowledge he had acquired. Strengthened by his own accolades, the scholar felt sure the Great Zen Master would grant his request. The Master listened patiently to every syllable the young scholar made, taking in every nuance, every fact and every weighted word proclaimed, and when the young scholar's speech finally subsided, he took a moment, and then offered the boy a cup of tea. How could the boy refuse? He was extraordinarily thirsty after his grand speech. When the tea was ready, and the cups set out empty and ready to be filled, the Zen Master lifted the pot and began to pour steaming water into the china, filling the cup.

The Zen Master held his hand steady and did not move. The water flowed over the rim of the cup, down its side and onto the table. Still the Master kept the water flowing. The water traced its way to the edge of the table and began its running, fast-flowing drip, eager to reach the floor and escape completely free and separate from the cup failing to contain it. The scholar, alarmed and puzzled by the lack of sight of the Great Zen Master, rose to his feet yelling, "Stop, stop, what are you doing? Can't you see the cup is full?" Still the Master kept the hot water flowing. "Stop!" The Scholar yelled, "Can't you see, the cup is full, you can't fit any more water in." The Great Zen Master calmly righted the pot and stopped pouring water into the overflowing cup. He sat down quietly, and when he knew he had the young Scholar's attention, he began: "You are like this cup. You are full of ideas about the Buddha's way. You proclaim all that you know, listing everything you have learned, proud of your own achievements, eager to show how much you know, and yet you come to me and ask for teachings. Your cup is overflowing. Before I can teach you anything, you are going to have to empty the cup. Only then are you ready to fully receive Zen."

Emptying the cup is a spiritual concept designed to aid you in understanding the need to let go of previous restrictive preconceptions and constructs that potentially limit your capacity to embrace your core *Truth* and connect with your innate spirituality. It is not simply a matter of emptying the cup in your mind; it requires you to address all aspects of life to embrace your full transformation and your *Awakening*. It is a place where the holistic symphony of *Body, Mind,* and *Spirit* unite in *Truth*, free from learned doctrine and humanized construct. This work, in its very nature, is often counterintuitive, as it is not only in the learning that you are transformed, but also in the unlearning that the *Truth* is revealed. Human beings are systematically and historically taught the understanding of our established physical world, primarily via text books, family beliefs, cultural patterns, and through the media. We are raised with linear, rational, and dogmatic practices. Spiritual recovery asserts a variant perception of life where you are responsible for your own limited belief system, ideas, opinions, and viewpoints, which often prevent you from gaining new wisdom. You are held prisoner by your own constructs.

When you release your perceptions, fixed ways of thinking, and your learned identities, you can feel as if you are jumping off a cliff, not knowing where or when you will land. You are often afraid to completely let go of something until the next best thing has presented itself. You get stuck, confused, frustrated, and sad; because you are attached to living inside a box despite knowing that there is an entirely different world to explore. You have the possibility of anything and everything, but first, you must be willing to have nothing at all. Divinity work leads to unleashing that which is already inside of you. It is the gemstone at the base of a cup, often lost and covered buried beneath a deceptive mirage of clutter.

The ultimate *Truth* is within; however, it cannot emerge until all the limited ideas which have lead you to perceive *"the way life is"* based on what you visually see and experience, are released and emptied from *Consciousness*. It is then that you are free to walk with the sages, saints, and mystics. As of today, you will begin to de-clutter, de-layer, and empty the cup, clearing out all aspects of your life that are limiting your *Consciousness*. You will let go of anything that is no longer serving your highest good, and you will surrender to the eternal and omnipotent here and now. If you master the ability to let go and learn to stop planning and thinking about what will come next, then a life experience beyond your wildest dreams will begin to emerge. Remember that at times, you will be inspired and supported by others. In other occasions, you will rely solely on yourself to take one giant leap of faith.

I was struck with a lightning bolt of inspiration watching, *The Edge of Never*, a documentary centered on the famous skier Trevor Peterson. In 1996, Trevor took an extreme skiing route in Chamonix, France, where an avalanche overpowered the acclaimed skiing mountaineer, and dragged him down the Glacier Rond's Exit Couloir, leaving his six-year-old son to grow up without a father. Nine years later at fifteen years of age, his little boy Kye bravely set out to ski the exact same mountain. Kye did not let fear or pain consume him; he stayed true to his love of skiing, loyal to his father's same love, and he excelled at what he was born to do. He became a playful, powerful, and most importantly, happy, world-renowned skier. It is an extraordinary story of rite of passage, and of the human spirit to persevere, displaying the essence and courage of the soul to transcend history. Spiritually speaking, when Kye successfully skied down the same mountain where his father had been killed, it transformed a previous tragedy into a resounding victory and a human triumph. The mountain, which once stood as a symbol of sadness, transformed into a symbol of glory.

In mythology, a rite of passage is a ritual or event marking a person's transcendence into maturity. We all have a mountain to conquer. We all have a horse to jump back on. We all have a battle that is not complete. When you overcome fear, you are doing it, not just for yourself, but for your entire heritage. When you rise to your Higher-Self and step into the shoes of grace, you take the entire human race with you, embracing the world and uniting it, in focused positive energy, expansion, and progress. We all have *The Edge of Never* inside of us, a moment, and a current and relevant choice to be conquered or to conquer. Fear is a product of the thoughts you create. While danger is real, fear is a choice. There are many talented people who have not fulfilled their dreams because they over-thought them, or they were too cautious and were unwilling to take the leap of faith. You do not have to be one of them. Choose to live in your point of power. Be in that place where you feel nervous, yet excited at the same time; that place where you release fear and stride out of your comfort zone and into the exhilaration of being fully alive. From there, you can begin to live outside of your box. You will enter a life of authentic ecstasy, inviting yourself to live boldly, without settling, and always radically dreaming.

Fear can affect you in multiple ways. There is not a single human on this planet that has not experienced it—fear of public speaking, fear of looking unattractive, fear of failure, fear of rejection, fear of getting out of your comfort zone, and even fear of success. The list goes on. Consider the two primary sources of

AWAKENING

fear: (a) being afraid of losing what you value, and (b) being afraid of not getting what you want. Interestingly, most people are more afraid to live fully than they are of dying. Humanity needs and wants your dreams and innovations to come true. Society wants you to thrive. It longs for your entertainment, art, passion, creativity, technology, and innovations to help the environment and scientific breakthroughs. We long to see thriving powerful human beings making a difference in the world. We long to see films that move us to tears and change our life perspective. We long for inventions that will help the paraplegic and end all cancer. We pray for the day where world hunger ends and world peace comes to fruition. Yet so many of us focus on the fear holding us back, allowing ourselves to be overwhelmed by it. I am here to tell you to do it anyway. When you feel afraid, it is not a sign to hold back, it is a time when it is even more necessary to act, to move forward, with every ounce of energy you can muster. The world needs and wants your dreams to come true. Fear is not only the opposite of faith; it is the exact energy that is opposing your dreams from manifesting.

Whether you consider yourself to be religious or spiritual, believe in something greater than you. Believe everything is vibrational energy. Faith is an unwavering belief in whatever you choose to believe in. When it comes to the metaphysics of faith, you must remember that your feelings inform the *Laws of the Universe* and the *Universe* responds accordingly. To have faith is to have utter and complete trust that your wants and desires are not just attainable, but are also your destiny.

When you have faith in yourself and in your dreams, there is zero room for fear or doubt and you know you will succeed. From a metaphysical or energetic standpoint, fear is an opposing energy or counter intention to what you are creating. When you generate fear, you are creating the opposing force against that which you are striving to manifest. Mastering your mind is the greatest skill of all.

Fear often lives within the constriction of your veins, brain, and your heart. Fear is the opposite of expanding; it is the retraction, disengagement, and exodus from fully living. It is the creation of disempowerment through assigning power to something outside of you to be more powerful than the force within.

Day 7 Practice

EMPTY YOUR CUP

LAW OF CORRESPONDENCE

This is the ascending order of the creative process; the spiritual realm to the mental realm to the physical realm. Your beliefs set this law into motion, creating the feelings, emotions, and circumstances of your life. Your ability to manifest and demonstrate is in direct correlation to your ability to provide a mental equivalent within your mind and soul. For every belief, there is an indistinguishable comparable in the physical form. The outer world is the reflection of the inner world, as within, so without.

Today's practice is to **EMPTY YOUR CUP!**

Look at your life today and identify which beliefs, viewpoints, and considerations no longer serve you.

> ➢ What beliefs have you filled your cup with that are not allowing new possibilities to come into your life?

> ➢ What limiting beliefs are you ready to let go of?

> ➢ What are your greatest fears? Fear of public speaking? Fear of being judged? Fear of failure? Fear of rejection? Fear of success?

> ➢ Which of these two do you fear the most:

Fear of losing what you value or fear of not getting what you want?

➢ What is the one thing, that if you did it, you would know you could do anything in this lifetime? Do it now. Mine was to write a book!

Day 8

Ego

We spend so much time on those résumé entries — entries that lose all significance as soon as our heart stops beating.

~ Arianna Huffington

There we were sitting overlooking the most spectacular view you could imagine; a three-hundred-and-fifty-degree scenic dream upon a hilltop at my client's house between Santa Barbara and Montecito: a multimillion dollar masterpiece. There was a full folding patio door system that left the entire front side of the home with an open face to the ocean. The interior and exterior beautifully meshed into one magnificent panoramic field of glorious vision. It was a picture-perfect dream home, worthy of a luxurious spread in any glossy design magazine.

After my client had given me the tour of his home, we sat down in two chairs that both faced out to the horizon. He slowly began to open up, sharing his vulnerability, revealing this epiphany, "The funny thing is that I don't look at the view anymore. I relate working and being isolated to this home now. I don't even want it anymore. I honestly don't care about any of this material stuff anymore." He turned his head, looking at me with a tear in his eye, and said, "Look, I realize that I've got to figure this whole thing out. As you know, I have an insurance company that has been thriving for over 27 years now. I have three homes, my kids are grown and doing great, but I can't get comfortable in my own skin. The feeling goes away for a moment here and there, when I'm golfing or on vacation, or when I drink a little at some social event, but it always returns. Something has got to change."

So many of us live our lives doing what we thought would make us happy. We took our parents' advice, went to the right school, got good grades, married the right person, had a child or two, lived in the right neighborhood, made plenty of money, and drove nice cars. For all intents and purposes, we are the pinnacle of success. We look like we have it all. So, it feels like we have been struck by an avalanche when we wake up one day and realize we never did anything we wanted to do. Our entire life we had been doing what the world and our ego told us to do.

I have two questions for you:

> Why is it that some people manifest everything they think they want and become more miserable than ever?
> In your heart of hearts, what does the word "successful" mean to you?

I have pondered those two questions for many years now and I have found clarity through understanding our spiritual nature. Until you *Awaken* and realize that true fulfillment, joy, abundance, vitality, prosperity, and love can only come from within, you will be lost in this world.

You are an infinite *Divine* Spiritual Being and you desire love, connection, and *Unique Divine Expression*. Yes, there are many people who create fame, fortune, or a considerable sum of money, but find themselves losing it all or becoming more depressed because they haven't found love and fulfillment within. We see it repeatedly; the rich person who commits suicide, the rock star that overdoses. People who seem to have it all are often the most miserable. We also see well-intended people that are unable to manifest what they think they want, leaving them frustrated and anxious. When it comes to reaching for dreams, the ego seeks validation, strives for superiority, or reaches for an identity to fulfill a void.

Others believe that it is as simple as changing their thinking, then they will change their lives, only to find themselves entangled in just another paradigm prison. Consider that nothing can truly change until you change your values, and the only true value shift happens through revelation of the Higher-Self.

Until you understand your spiritual nature you will be ruled by the ego; battling with yourself in a never-ending war where nothing is gained and everything is lost. Until you value yourself enough and believe in yourself unconditionally, without needing proof of your worth, you will often be looking to fulfill a perpetual and seemingly bottomless abyss.

The body has a built-in intelligence system that knows authentic bliss from ego-driven endeavors. There is a link among *Body*, *Mind* and *Spirit* within each of us at our solar plexus that communicates via our gut instinct. *Spirit* signals to let you know when you are in alignment with your Higher-Self or not. Like a

GPS system, through intuition, elevated *Consciousness* signals each cell of our body toward self-expression and love. The body is all knowing and wise beyond measure. When you hand over your thinking to this intelligence, you begin to experience true wellness. Today, honor your physical body. It knows.

Day 8 Practice

LEAN IN

LAW OF DIVINITY

You are a spiritual being governed by Universal Laws. The extent to which you unite with the indwelling Divine source and expand your Consciousness is the extent to which you will experience Divinity and being a revealer of Truth. Your true identity is a Divine expression of the One. You are capable of direct revelation of Truth through your intuition and spiritual nature.

Today's practice is to **LEAN IN:**

➢ What if you leaned in today in all areas of your life, giving your heart unconditionally and unboundedly?

➢ What if you walked through life not needing any validation, not needing to be liked, not needing acceptance from anyone?

➢ What if you gave love, even when it didn't feel like it was being reciprocated?

➢ What if you stayed in your *Divine* connected nature, instead of acting divided and withdrawing from life?

Day 9

Upsets and Justifications

Your beliefs become your thoughts, your thoughts become your words, your words become your actions, your actions become your habits, your habits become your values, your values become your destiny.

~Mahatma Gandhi

Consider this: Do you think it is worse to eat a candy bar or get upset? Have you ever felt the effects of fear, anger, deceit, resentment, sadness, turmoil, or grief running through your veins? The candy bar and the upset both amount to one and the same as far as your *Body*, *Mind*, and *Spirit* are concerned: *Stress*.

Stress may be the most toxic feeling you can ever manifest because there is an abundance of it waiting to be excreted through the unlimited misuse of your mind. It is very simple to break down where stress and upsets come from. Your thoughts are created through your beliefs and what you value. You attach positive or negative meaning to things and experiences which instantaneously evoke feelings. Your feelings create emotions, decisions, actions, and eventually build the circumstances around you. From a metaphysical standpoint, this process can happen instantaneously, or in a linear format depending on the beliefs that back the entire process. Ultimately, you are the only source that is responsible for the stress you feel.

As Dan Millman says, "Suffering is our psychological resistance to what happens. Events may create physical pain, but they do not in themselves create suffering. Resistance creates suffering. Stress happens when your mind resists what is. The only problem in your life is your mind's resistance to life as it unfolds." Your body becomes the victim of your stressful mind. Your limited thinking, your set ways, your expectations, and your misplaced values and emotions can cause havoc on every organ of your body, making your blood pressure rise and planting cancerous seeds. You can blame others, speak of broken promises, expectations, victim stories, but the reality is that nothing can cause stress except the way you think. To take responsibility and respond in a positive manner no matter what occurs in life is a sure measure of how *Awakened* someone is. This does not mean you keep putting your hands back into a flame that keeps burning you, or stay in any circumstance where negative reactions are inevitable. This means you make positive choices and create a life where you can stay in serenity, no matter what.

Within you lives a mythical story just itching to surface and ruin your day. There is always an extensive list of reasons as to why you cannot achieve your dreams. You can keep recanting this silly story, or you can look toward heroic people such as Helen Keller, who had every justification in the world to forget her dreams, yet chose to seize destiny with her own hands. In 1882, at 19 months old, she fell ill with a terrible fever, which left her blind, deaf, and mute. This was a time in history before Braille or any tools had been invented for the blind or the deaf.

She was left to struggle within, without any portal to communicate with the outside world. With the help of her dear teacher, Anne Sullivan, Helen slowly learned how to communicate with one person, breaking through and unleashing her inner strength and *Spirit*. She became the first blind individual to earn a Bachelor of Arts degree. She also published her autobiography at the age of 22 and was the subject of the movie *The Miracle Worker*. Moreover, she proceeded to write six additional books ("American," n.d.). Helen remains a world-famous and historical icon. Her story is a testimony of the potential of a determined mind and *Spirit* to become magnificent. Within each of us lives the potential of a new story of grace, victory, and glory. As Helen Keller stated, "life is either a daring adventure or nothing at all."

A justification is just another word for an excuse. It is a reason, a fact, a circumstance, or an explanation that upholds or defends one's disempowerment. You use justifications to explain why you are late, why you are bored, why you are miserable, why you are not living your dreams, why you are depressed, why you are not financially stable, and overall, why you feel negative emotions. Justifications can come in many forms. For example, "I did not get you that report because you said you would let me know when you wanted to meet, but you never told me; therefore, I didn't do the report." Or, "I did not call you because I did not know what time to call because you said you were busy, even though I said I would call." Or, "I was late for the meeting because there was traffic," as if you are unable to plan or take traffic possibilities into consideration. If you wait for the entire world to show up perfectly for you to be who you want to be, you will die not living the life you are truly designed to live.

Justifications serve as some of the most disempowering messages that you send yourself because they assign power outside of you. For example, when you make an excuse and justify that you do not have enough time or money, you trap yourself into being less powerful than those circumstances. You become an effect of this world. You are telling your *Subconscious* that money and time are more powerful than the *Spirit* within. Through your free will, you will either build a case as to why you are not able to become your greatest self, or a case as to why you have been successful at doing so. The *Truth* is that you are infinite potential, beyond your wildest dreams. As you take full accountability of your life by giving up justifications, excuses, and victim rationalization, you can and will begin your *Awakening*!

Empty Your Cup of Justifications

Step One: Observe your justifications. As you go through your day or your week, notice when you explain why you did something. Take note of the justifications you use to make yourself and your choices right. Justifications may not seem important, but they are extremely dis-empowering. They are like little cracks in concrete that end up destroying the entire foundation of a house that then must be torn down and rebuilt.

Step Two: Take 100% responsibility. If you want to unleash the guru within, then you must intentionally speak your world into existence. If I declare myself less powerful than money, another person, situation, or circumstance, then I instantaneously create myself to be less powerful than it. An effortless way to reclaim your power is to take full responsibility for your actions. Example, "I was late because I didn't take traffic into consideration. From now on I will make sure to schedule in more time for driving in case there is traffic."

Step Three: Reclaim your power. Shift your mind from needing to prove why you cannot do something to why you can do something. This paradigm shift is the Taekwondo of the mental game of living a powerful life. When you can begin to turn obstacles into opportunities, you can begin to have breakthroughs out of the breakdowns. Stop justifying why you are not creating what you want in life and begin declaring why you are creating what you desire in your life. Start talking about how unstoppable you are, how success is your destiny, how you decide, and so it is!

Day 9 Practice

BREAK THROUGH YOUR REACTIONS

LAW OF POLARITY

The Law of Polarity is set into motion by Spirit (Your Higher-Self) contemplating its own identity. The moment you consider something to be, it sets Universal Laws into motion. Beliefs within the soul activate and direct energy. Also, intention, attention, initiation, and selection set the mechanics into motion.

Today's practice is to **BREAK THROUGH YOUR REACTIONS**!

Begin to see the opportunity in the breakdowns, transforming your viewpoint and setting the law into motion through the polarity of your soul.

The shift is to view all *upsets* as the opportunity to do your own spiritual work, peeling back the layers of the onion within the mind. Use each mishap as an opportunity to expand your *Consciousness* and empty the cup of all the things that are holding you back from your *Divinity*.

When anxiety and stress surface, feel the ground beneath your feet and monitor your breathing, allowing long slow breaths to carry oxygen to every cell in your body. Deep breathing always connects you to *Source*, helping you to stay present and better able to find the serenity in every situation. Ask yourself the following questions:

➢ What is or is not occurring that is causing me to feel upset or stressed?

➢ What expectations do I have that are not happening?

➢ What is or is not occurring in the circumstances of my life that is having me label or assign a negative meaning?

➢ What beliefs or values do I have that are not being met?

➢ Are these beliefs true, or are they stories I have made up in my mind?

➢ Am I willing to let go of my limited beliefs and accept the situation as it is or am I willing to change myself?

Remember that you cannot change another person, circumstance, or thing; you can only alter your *Consciousness*.

Day 10

Limited Beliefs

Step out of the history that is holding you back. Step into the new story you are willing to create.

~ Oprah Winfrey

The Wright brothers believed they could build an airplane and because of their belief, the very first flight took place on December 17, 1903. Steve Jobs believed he could create the most technologically advanced phone in history, and through his vision, the iPhone was born. Ada Lovelace believed she could program a machine with mathematical algorithms and because of her determination, the first computer was programmed. Solar-power pioneer, Dr. Maria Telkes believed she could heat a home entirely by solar power, and the very first 'solar only' home was built in 1947. Edwin Hubble believed man could go to the moon, and through his perseverance, he invented the famous Hubble space telescope—the impetus to space travel. There are as many potential creations as there are stars in all the galaxies in the *Universe*. This is infinity. There are as many beliefs as any man or woman can create. They can take us to the moon or they can box us into our own prison cell. It is the use of the creative substance, which determines if you expand your expression or inhibit yourself. Limited beliefs create filters of what you allow to flow and manifest in your life.

The entire physical and material world is made up of the substance of form, which is created by the intelligence of *Consciousness*, informing and directing energy into matter. And just as matter is created, so too is the experience of life through your perceptions. Your viewpoint is individualized through the constraints of limited beliefs within your *Consciousness*. However, you not only affect your experience through your limited beliefs, you create the circumstances of your life. Energy is 99.9% empty space that is informed by the observer that collapses the energy into either a wave, or particle, much like a binary code to the entire matrix.

All universal matter is vibrational; a vibrational communicating intelligence which informs matter to form structure. Your circumstances are a direct result of your feelings, which are a direct result of your thoughts, which are a direct result of your beliefs. Your beliefs are the single most powerful tool you have, which create either a heaven or hell in your life. Beliefs can either destroy or create your dreams. As you begin to expand your mind and let go of limiting beliefs, you naturally feel wellness within your body. Your stress levels begin to lower and your love levels begin to rise. This phenomenon assists in lifting not only your *Spirit*, but physically, it raises your serotonin levels and energetic vibration. You can begin to exhale and navigate life in your newfound oneness.

Quantum physics demonstrates the field of potentiality and the effect of your individual *Consciousness* on matter in the physical realm. Science has proven that all matter in its unobserved state is both particle and wave. It is through your observation that the energy takes form, dictated by your vibration. Dr. Fred Allen Wolf, otherwise known as Dr. Quantum, is a famous physicist who has boldly stated that *Consciousness* creates the physical world and that the *Universe* does not exist without a perceiver of that *Universe (Wolf, n.d.)*.

The first step in emptying the *Consciousness* of limited beliefs is to become aware of what limited beliefs you have. The next step is to actively choose which beliefs you would like to discard and which ones you would like to keep. Practicing compassion and patience is imperative through this process because often when you begin to observe your limited beliefs, it opens a Pandora's Box within the mind. The fractals go deep into the *Subconscious* and further into the entire life matrix, and it can be overwhelming.

It is time to stop your unconstructive ways of thinking that are holding you back from the all-powerful beautiful *Divine* being that you are. You need to release your limited beliefs and acknowledge the *Truth* of who you are; an abundant, spiritual being, and infinite innovator that has the potential to *Awaken*. No matter what the belief, it can be changed. There is always infinite room for growth. Metaphysically, the moment you change your beliefs, your entire experience of life, including your perception of your past, alters. Emptying the *Consciousness* changes your history. When you change your beliefs, you change your story of the past, the present, and the future. According to the teachings of the *Wheel of Samsara*, when we heal ourselves, we heal our ancestry seven generations in each direction. It is through your thinking that you can liberate yourself and your lineage from all suffering. You are not your beliefs; you are the believer. You are not your thoughts; you are the thinker. You are not your feelings; you are the creator of the meaning that brings forth the feelings.

Day 10 Practice

BECOME FASCINATED BY PEOPLE'S BELIEFS

LAW OF DIVINE WILL

The absolute Truth is that God's will is your will. This law works in direct proportion to your ability to direct energy upon Universal Law by the power of your mind and the conviction of your heart. Divine Will has nothing to do with using force upon the physical realm. Control is influenced by the beliefs within your soul.

Today's practice is to **BECOME FASCINATED BY PEOPLE'S BELIEFS!**

➢ Notice other people's beliefs.

➢ How do they view the world, what do they think is right or wrong?

➢ What do they think other people should do? What limited beliefs do they have?

➢ How do they perceive themselves to be? Start to become aware of what people focus on due to their own beliefs.

➢ Do they find life difficult or easy?

➢ Do they find faults in the opposite sex?

➢ Do they view life as mundane or miraculous?

As you contemplate human beings and the world this way, become fascinated. If after observing people's beliefs you have a desire to correct them, do not. Just notice them and become fascinated by what they are creating for themselves. Begin to pick and choose which beliefs in your life you would like to keep and which ones you would like to get rid of. Feel the freedom!

Day 11

Indecision

Waiting is painful. Forgetting is painful. But not knowing which to do is the worst kind of suffering.

~Paulo Coelho

One time I had a client who came to me for spiritual counseling. She felt paralyzed mentally and was completely overwhelmed with life. She had days where she couldn't even decide what to eat for dinner. At one point, she perceived every choice as permanent for the rest of her life. Rather than choosing incorrectly, she decided to stop making decisions all together. Her life began to fall apart. Her relationship with her boyfriend ended, she got fired from her job, and her health began to decline.

Indecision, procrastination, and lack of commitment are silent monsters for many people. All choices have consequences. Many people flitter-flatter through life being noncommittal and jumping from one thing to the next, never seeing things through, always certain to never stay too long in fear that they will miss out on other options. They go around in circles, never choosing a destination, or they start-and-stop projects over and over again, never completing cycles. Ironically, this behavior ensures exactly what that person fears the most. Life backs them into a corner where they must make a choice.

Choice does not equal more freedom. Schwartz, in *The Paradox of Choice*, maintains that too many choices causes you to have lofty expectations, and it is these expectations that lead to disappointment. He discusses how even going to purchase grocery items can be difficult, with 285 varieties of cookies, 75 iced teas, 230 soups, 175 different salad dressings, and 40 different types of toothpaste. He also mentions how overwhelming it can be to buy a stereo when he researches for one and realized there are 6.5 million varieties (Schwartz, 2009). We live in the technical information age that has left some of us paralyzed by choice. They say knowledge is power, but we have trained our brains to have attention deficit by multitasking, such as texting while driving, internet browsing while dining with friends, working and checking personal emails, and chatting on Facebook during meetings. The list goes on. Even getting a coffee requires a minimum of three choices. Do you want it iced, hot, organic, skinny, sugar-free, short, tall, Grande, Venti, double shot, steamed milk, half-caf, blended, latte, cappuccino, with cream, sprinkles? The options at Starbucks can seem infinite.

We strive for freedom in our culture, yet the exact thing we want so often is the exact thing which prevents us from obtaining it. Where indecision abides, displeasure, disruption, and anxiety pervades.

We want a lightning bolt to come out of the sky and strike us with clarity, erasing all confusion, bringing us definitive answers to our questions. We strive for certainty even though nothing in our *Universe* is absolute. You want to know what to do with your life? Your only job is to follow your bliss and enjoy the journey.

Consider that saying that you do not know what you want is just another pretense. You are pretending. Not knowing is another lie you are telling yourself. It is another internal obstacle holding you back from your true self. It is the con artist that lives inside of you. Stop it. Stop telling yourself this lie. You know what you like and what you do not like. The *Universe* only knows *yes*, so if you send it mixed messages via indecision, it must reflect to you mixed messages and more confusing signs.

THE ONLY OPPONENT IS YOURSELF

Say yes to the things you love; say yes to the passions you have; say yes to only spending time on things that speak to your heart; say yes to the commitment you made for yourself; say yes to staying focused, no matter what, to the things you want to accomplish; say yes to exciting events and extraordinary people; say yes to making every moment intentional and memorable.

Day 11 Practice

DEMAND YOUR 'MUST HAVES'

LAW OF EMERGENT EVOLUTION

During evolution, upon demand for life to prevail, there emerges new properties. For example; the fifth finger emerged out of necessity for survival. Form transforms upon insistence of Consciousness. When the individual demands and commands the subconscious and subjective mind, the Universal Laws are set into motion.

Today's practice is to **DEMAND YOUR 'MUST HAVES'!**

Begin to say 'no' to the things that don't speak to your heart and say 'yes' to the things that make your heart sing.

➤ What must you have in your relationships?
➤ What must you have for your health?
➤ What must you have financially?
➤ What must you have to be self-expressive?

Now, ask yourself:
➤ Am I willing to do what it takes to obtain my must haves?
➤ What wisdom do I need to embody to be the person equivalent to having this life?

Day 12

Secrets, Lies and Withholds

*Above all, don't lie to yourself. The man who lies to himself and
listens to his own lie comes to a point that he cannot distinguish the
Truth within him, or around him, and so loses all respect for himself
and for others. And having no respect he ceases to love.*

~Fyodor Dostoyevsky

In Paul Guay's strikingly accurate film *Liar Liar*, Jim Carrey
plays a lying, cheating lawyer named Fletcher Reede, who
believes lying is just part of winning the game of life. He lies in
court, he lies to women, he lies to his son, and he lies all day long.
He can't stop lying. After not showing up to his son's birthday,
and lying about why, his son makes one wish: that his dad will
not be able to tell any lies for an entire day. So, the next day,
Reed wakes up unable to say anything but the truth. The day
turns into a disaster, as he exposes his true thoughts, but as the
day progresses it gets easier and easier. The beautifully crafted
and hilarious message shines through the course of the movie,
making the point that being truthful is difficult, but it always
harvests the greatest results. We long to live truthful lives; it is
naturally empowering. Lying remains the antithesis to your
spiritual practice, which incarcerates *Spirit* and hinders our own

creation. Ricky Gervais, in the movie *The Invention of Lying,* similarly makes a valid point regarding the human need for *Truth.* This film delves into chaos and reveals that lying is a man-made invention. We are constantly bombarded with various belief systems being thrust upon us through media, politics, corporation propaganda, and culture. We are all jettisoned in the middle of the desert dying of thirst, as it is not water that we need for survival; we desperately need *Truth*!

Ayn Rand states, "People think that a liar gains victory over his victim. What I've learned is that a lie is an act of self-abdication, because one surrenders one's reality to the person to whom one lies, making that person one's master, condemning oneself from then on to faking the sort of reality that persons view requires to be faked. The man who lies to the world is the world's slave from then on. There are no white lies, there is only the blackest of destruction and a white lie is the blackest of all."

Lying is a fascinating topic when it comes to understanding cause and effect and how the *Law of the Universe* works. *The Universe* functions in direct correlation to your actions. What you put out comes back, and what you sow, so shall you reap. When you lie, you essentially remove another person's power of choice based on *Truth*, and when this occurs, the person who lies rejects and surrenders his or her own free will. That's right. The person who lies throws away his or her own power through the action of lying. What is lied about retains the power. For example, if you lie about alcohol, drugs, or sex, you end up becoming powerless over the exact thing which you lied about, sacrificing your integrity, surrendering your power to the exact thing you lied about.

The first step in Alcoholics Anonymous' 12-step program is admitting that one is powerless over alcohol. As good and pure spirits, we know deep down inside that lying is an anti-survival action. You pinch yourself away from your *Truth* by lying.

Awakening allows the continual sacred space to have your own personal *Truth* revealed. Being truthful allows you to get in touch with your authenticity, able to feel your body as an indicator of what feels true for you. When you begin to live in alignment with your *Truth*, genuine love emerges through your spiritual *Awakening*. You find liberation in living transparent and authentic lives. Your relationships become the opportunity to practice your principles of being genuine and intentional. You move past the ego into the heart, releasing any fear of rejection. Each time you are faced with a choice, there is a little indicator within a solar plexus that signals a yes or no. When you honor your *Truth*, you feel peace within your body, your stress levels drop, and your energy is freed up to heal and experience true vitality. Your body literally thrives on *Truth* and deteriorates with secrets, lies, and withholds.

Day 12 Practice

BE TRANSPARENT

LAW OF KARMA

Karma is the sum of the actions of the Individual, Collective, and Cosmic Consciousness. This includes all lifetimes, all creation, and all thinking. Everything that exists has come from Spirit and each person is living out his or her specific lineage karma. The extent to which the Collective uses the life force for harmony is the extent we will create heaven on earth and vice versa. The disease factors caused from genetics are the sum of the actions upon that lineage. New karma is created via new thinking and new actions.

Today's practice is to **BE TRANSPARENT!**

Take ten minutes to journal, taking inventory of where you are in life.

- ➤ What secrets, lies, and withholds do you carry?

- ➤ What are the negative costs and what is the impact these have on your life and the people within your life?

- ➤ Where in life do you lie to yourself?

- ➤ What are you willing to do to clean up your lies and take responsibility for living a transparent life?

Day 13

Problems

*You do not have a problem except the one that is in your own mind,
and you put it there!*

~Myrtle Fillmore

When I was fifteen, I remember thinking that once I turned sixteen I would finally be happy because I would be able to drive and be completely free and independent. On my sixteenth birthday, I raced out and bought my first car with the money I had saved from waiting tables in a local restaurant. I was quickly brought back to reality as my car continuously kept breaking down. I thought I would finally be happy when I could afford a brand-new car. I worked and worked and saved and saved and eventually had enough money to put a down payment on a new car. Along came a new problem: my car payment was stressful because it was more than I could afford. I thought I would be happy when I finally could make enough money to cover my car payment comfortably, so I worked on getting a better paying job, with the opportunity to work longer hours to make more money. Then I was miserable because I was working all the time.

We often believe that if we just solve our current problem, we will be happy and life will work out. This is not true; in fact, it is one of the biggest misconceptions known to man. One thing you may often fail to notice is that every circumstance is a stepping stone leading to something much greater.

The shift within, the *Awakening*; it is the key that unlocks our ability to transform problems into opportunities. Have you ever noticed that people get attached to their problems? It is as if they are addicted to an emotional rollercoaster of highs and lows and ups and downs. Problems can become a recurring theme if you are not careful where your attention lies. Identifying yourself with your problems is one of the most disempowering actions you can engage in. You do it in many forms; sometimes you may keep playing the same drama over and over in your relationships, in your finances, and in your head. You may even have reoccurring family problems or issues with your boss at work. You should be wary of using problems as excuses not to be happy.

Your number one priority is to let go of resistance and transform problems into opportunities. Look for a way to clear the road-blocks and move forward in every area of your life. Problems are the opportunity for your soul to declare to the *Universe* and to yourself what you are committed to, allowing you to stop identifying yourself through the circumstances of your life. They help to bring you clarity regarding what it is you want, and what you do not want.

You can use the times when you are volatile, over reactive, or upset, as an opportunity to step into your grace and either accept what is, or expand your *Consciousness* and act to change yourself. Ignorance is not bliss; it is the opportunity to seek wisdom. Where there is despair, there is hope. Where there is division there is *Divinity*. Life always presents opportunity for growth.

In order to find solutions to your problems, you must change the way you view them, as you cannot solve them with the same thinking that created them. What if you viewed problems as opportunities for growth? What if you took the time to see your life advances, leading to greater manifestations, showing you that you are exactly where you need to be and headed to more incredible things. Instead of focusing on problems, take a moment to be grateful and appreciative for all that you have. Then you will see your life magically transform and a flow of abundance come your way. Happiness, fulfillment, and peace only come from one source: *Within*. Worry, stress, and angst are only giving energy to the circumstances of your life. Gandhi believed that if you want to solve your problems, make better problems. Unless you are starving, do not have shelter, or have a health issue beyond your control, then most so-called problems are justifications to avoid living life to the fullest. I ask you, what is the better problem? To some it may be solving world hunger, and for others, it may be creating a life they love.

Day 13 Practice

FIND PERFECTION IN THE IMPERFECTION

LAW OF PERFECTION

At a spiritual level, there is only perfection. There is Divine order to the cosmos and a harmonic progression within every cause and effect. Life is unfolding perfectly. You are whole and complete exactly as you are. Perfect God - Perfect Man - Perfect Being. There is a perfect mental equivalent to everything created in the physical Universe designed for your Awakening.

Today's practice is to **FIND PERFECTION IN THE IMPERFECTION!**

➤ What problems are constantly playing in your mind?

➤ What recurring themes of problems keep showing up in your life?

➤ What do you keep doing over and over, hoping for a different outcome?

➤ Take ten minutes to brainstorm on how you could transform your problems into opportunities.

Day 14

Complaining

Imagine who we would be if we were complaint free. If only one percent of the population was complaint free, we would have the courage to love. I think war would be laughed out of the room. Just imagine, people would speak kinder to each other. We would care more about the children. We would love everyone...Black, Jewish, the Chinese, the homeless, your neighbor. We would no longer blame anyone. We could touch each other. It would be just the beginning of paradise. Nothing can dim the light which shines from within.

~ Maya Angelou

A girlfriend of mine was concerned because she was planning on spending the weekend with her mom, but was worried because she said that her mother often complained and played the victim, and she was not sure how she was going to handle it. She posted on social media, seeking advice from many of her friends on how to handle this situation. Some suggested she should try to empathize with her mother, others said she should set her boundaries, and some said she should counsel her.

My friend decided to have a genuine conversation and talk about her issues with her mother. The weekend came, and after a couple of days with her mom, she realized that her mother's core belief was feeling worthless. My friend also realized that she had a similar belief: *I am not enough*. She said, "Today, while counseling my mother, I've discovered that thinking that *I am not enough* is a step up from my mother's belief that she is worthless. That day she had a life changing realization and no longer would ever be able to view someone who complains in the same way. She understood that others often complain out of a place of inadequacy. She felt a rush of compassion for her mother.

Consider that all complaints are a projection of your frustration and dis-empowerment within. All negative feelings that you experience are projected outward into the world of circumstances, creating the illusion that you are separate from all of life.

WHEN YOU COMPLAIN, IT IS LIKE PRAYING FOR CRAP

It is not fun to be around someone who complains all the time, let alone listen to your own self-denouncing voice within. You observe the paradoxical phenomenon *you spot it, you got it.* If you complain about someone complaining, is that not the same thing? The difference may be when someone is seeking constructive advice on how to act around a situation. The best situation is to find someone who gives good advice, holding you responsible for raising your own *Consciousness*, without a need to change you. Complaining is a sickness that is contagious through the mirroring cells of the mind or a lineage in our DNA.

YOU SPOT IT, YOU GOT IT

We all do it. We complain about people, places, and things. Complaining about how hard life is, complaining about what our mother did, complaining about the line at the grocery store, complaining about our boss, complaining about how much a dinner costs, complaining about our husband/wife, complaining about what our friend did, complaining about everything.

There must be a payoff. Is there something people get out of making people, places, and things wrong? Or is it just another decoy from having to fully step into our power, grace, and Higher-Selves? The issue with complaining is that when you pretend to be the effect of a circumstance or person, you designate the cause to be out in the world, and become powerless. People sit around complaining, ranting, and raving, falling into a pity party of victimhood, as if it solves a problem. It is the antithesis to empowerment. It is like a virus that takes hold of the psyche, dis-empowering and 'duping' the self into believing it is different, separate, and alone. Next time you hear someone complain, you may consider becoming more compassionate and giving a little more love.

A Silly Story

There once was a construction worker who had a habit of complaining. Monday at noon he opened his lunch bag and took in the fresh smell of his sumptuous baloney sandwich which he enjoyed during his lunch break. On Tuesday at noon, he opened his lunch bag again and lo and behold another baloney sandwich appeared before him. Slight annoyance swept over him as he took his first bite, resenting the lack of surprise and utter predictability his sandwich offered. On Wednesday at noon, guess what happened. He saw the very same sandwich again. He was furious; how was it that he had to put up with the same crap every day. He worked hard, he was a good man, and surely, he deserved something to look forward to on his break! Not the same old miserable, predictable lunch he got every single day. Now he began to complain, "Another baloney sandwich?!!!" Thursday came and once again he screamed, "Another baloney sandwich? If I see this thing again tomorrow I may have to kill myself!" Friday, the same thing happened and as he kept screaming, "A baloney sandwich, another baloney sandwich!" One of his coworkers overheard his moans and yelled at him a clear, level-headed response that would obviously solve the problem. "Hey, why don't you tell your wife to stop packing all these baloney sandwiches for you? Communicate and stop your whining." This advice did not rest easy with the man. In fact, it angered him even more. Now he had a boring lunch and someone giving him a challenging time. The construction worker took offense. What on earth was this guy's problem? Unbelievable! He would not stand for that and he yelled back fiercely and with pride." Hey, you leave my wife out of this! You hear! You leave my wife out of this! I pack my own lunch!" This joke by Brian Randham sends the simple message to stop complaining. Change what you're doing! Realize your own power, influence, and choice.

We have the choice to be the victim and complain, or we can be the solution by focusing on what we do want to create. Complaining will never get us what we want as it will simply get us more of what we don't want. What we give our attention to is what the *Universe* delivers to us. You create your entire world into existence through the way you speak it into existence. Metaphysics teaches us to miraculously speak our relationships into existence through constructive thoughts. By viewing people as the miracles that they are instead of complaining about them, you create a space allowing them to view their own potential. You inspire them into creating what you desire for them by seeing them in the most positive of lights. When you are aligned with your own *Truth*, you have the power to positively influence those around you, and when you envision and focus on the best in them, then the best is them is what the *Universe* delivers to you. You stand for, endorse, and promote their *Divinity*. From an energetic standpoint, when you focus on someone complaining, you help support the persistence of it.

Day 14 Practice

100% COMPLAINT-FREE

LAW OF RECIPROCITY

The Universe is a quantum field, where everything is connected. There is a mutual dependence, action, and exchange between you and the Universe. You get what you give and you reap what you sow. Whatever you send to the cosmos, whether it's good or bad, must be returned. This is the Law of Mutual Exchange. Therefore, every action has an equal and opposite reaction. Life is like playing a game of Ping-Pong. Whatever you give to life is returned to you and multiplies abundantly.

Today's practice is to be **100% COMPLAINT-FREE** for 24 hours!

Practice Non-Complaining

➤ Be gentle on yourself and others through this process. Keep the faith that over time, your entire life as you know it will alter into a world beyond your recognition. Complaining contracts the heart and stresses the mind, creating acid and toxins in the veins. When you are ready to have abundant energy and vibrant vitality, you will detox from complaining.

➤ Live a complaint-free life and avoid talking about people behind their back, unless it is to say how wonderful they are. Stop your complaining mentality and start your solution mentality. This can be one of the biggest game changers to transforming your life, yet, one of the most challenging. If you have been someone who has gotten into negative arguments with friends for most your life, the ability to stop complaining can be perceived as extraordinarily challenging; however, that is a limited belief. You can let go of complaining the moment you commit to it.

➤ This exercise is simple; pay close attention to your thoughts and focus on them. The moment you hear yourself complaining or getting into negative discussions with others, switch the focus toward what you are grateful for about that person or that circumstance. If in that moment, it is too difficult to find something about your circumstance to be grateful about, find non-related things to be thankful for.

➤ Remember, it may take some time to get into the habit of switching your focus. Do not beat yourself up if you do not do it perfectly at first. It is a skill that must be practiced every moment of your day. You may be thinking, "Well this sounds easy, but what if my friend complains all the time or constantly engages in negative talk?" Find solutions for this question. Have a heart-to-heart conversation informing your friends that you are committed to no longer complaining and to support you in this endeavor; walk away from situations that create negative thoughts and feelings; find ways to distract from negativity. Eventually, this task will become easier and easier as you continue to practice it and incorporate it into your everyday life.

Day 15

Scarcity Mentality

Man's chief delusion is his conviction that there are causes other than his own state of consciousness.

~Neville

Dr. John Demartini is considered one of the leading human behaviorist and personal development speakers today. One day he was taking a flight from Phoenix to Las Vegas. He sat down next to a pretty girl who proceeded to ask him about his travels. He told her he was on his way to give a seminar about manifesting all the things you want out of life. She asked if he would advise her on her own love life. She said she loved her life, but was unable to figure out the love part. Intrigued and ever helpful, he took the time on the flight to listen and to help her. He asked her to tell him about the men that were in her life and to discuss the qualities she liked about each of them. She talked about her boss and how he just adored and spoiled her and her friends. He would take her and her friends out to dinners and fun events. She told of her hair dresser and how he made her laugh hysterically. She began to tell him how she was still intimate with her ex-boyfriend who was so sexually compatible it felt like a dream, but he did not match up in other aspects of their life. As she went on, the speaker enlightened her and opened her eyes at the abundance she was experiencing in her life. He talked about how the *Universe* always gives us everything we need; it is our perception of how we attain the things we want that limits our ability to see what we have. He reiterated how she had every whim, need, and desire already fulfilled. He told her that she could find all that she wants in one person, but first, she needs to acknowledge and give gratitude for the abundance she already has. She had an epiphany, realizing for the first time how wonderful everything in her life was, exhaling with gratitude.

All of life is energy. When you create a negative or positive reaction to something, there is an equal and opposite reaction. When you use your mind to direct energy away from abundance, you bind yourself. When decisions are made from a point of scarcity, such as lack, fear, angst, separation, or victimhood, the mind instantaneously creates those exact equations. It is profoundly important to step into the physics of thinking. Focusing on problems creates more problems, whereas creating from a mindset of gratitude generates ecstatic opportunity. Bliss and angst are identical in that they are both generated from the *One Energy Source, Consciousness*, and both are created from the sequence of events of your thinking. Beliefs create thoughts, thoughts create feelings, feelings create emotions, and emotions create the experience of life.

Through your understanding of the laws, you can either create scarcity or abundance, as both are created from the same energy. You either block or allow the abundance through your thinking patterns. It is so much easier when you focus on abundance, because what you resist persists; if you focus on what you do not have, you will get more of *not having*.

When you finally DECIDE, choose to focus, act, and create abundance through The *Law of Correlation* and Newton's Third Law, the *Universe* will have to reflect exactly what you feed it. The moment you see life through the lens of scarcity, your body automatically feels negative emotions such as angst, sadness, loneliness, and despair. Over time, those prolonged thoughts and feelings compound and can have an adverse and direct impact on your physical health, leading to depression, heart disease, and many other illnesses.

The *Universe* always gives you what you need, and whether it is in the form of a lesson or a blessing, it is all in the form of love. The *Universe* nudges you towards your *Awakening*. The paradigm shift and Spiritual Principle is realizing that there is only abundance in the *Universe*. There is an infinite number of ways that prosperity comes your way in this moment in time; all you have to do is open your eyes, your mind, and your heart to allow yourself to receive them.

Day 15 Practice

FOCUS ON GRATITUDE

LAW OF EVOLUTION

The creative process begins with a belief in mind, which sets polarity into motion. Evolution is the result of this polarity in physical form. Involution is the internal impression upon mind and what informs Universal Law. Evolution is the outcome of the law in motion, which affects the elements and chemical reactions.

Today's practice is to **FOCUS ON GRATITUDE!**

Pick one of the following:

➢ Write down twenty things you are grateful for.

➢ Write a letter of gratitude to someone.

➢ Make a phone call to someone you are grateful for and let that person know the things you appreciate about him or her.

Day 16

Someday

Perfection is achieved, not when there is nothing more to add, but when there's nothing left to take away.

~Antoine de Saint-Exupery

One day, a middle-aged woman came to me quite confused and down. She said, "I think I'm having a mid-life crisis, but I don't know why." She went on to explain, "My life is okay, I have a decent marriage, a nice house, my kids are healthy, and nothing is wrong with me physically." After diving a bit deeper, she came to realize that she had become apathetic to life and wasn't excited about anything any longer. Her entire life she lived for *someday*. She thought when she grew up and moved out of her parent's house, she would be happy. Then, she thought once she was done with college, she would be happy. Then, she thought once she made enough money in her career, she should be happy. Then, she thought once she got married, she would be happy. Then, she thought she would be happy when she and her husband were able to buy the house of their dreams. Then, she thought she would be happy when they had children. Everything she wished for happened, but guess what, she never was happy. Her entire happiness was attached to an image of *someday*. She didn't realize that what was driving her was the belief that someday, some image of life was going to complete her.

When we are children, we are constantly creating and imagining our future adult world. Make believe, dress up, and play all help us to emulate a fantastical world of our future *someday*. Maybe you dreamt of falling in love, having a family, becoming successful, and living a rich, fulfilling, and abundant life. Or maybe you dreamt of becoming an actor, an artist, a fire fighter, or a professional dancer. Then you grew up and you kept playing the same game, only you did not realize you were still playing it. You stopped calling it *make believe* or *dress up*, but nonetheless, that same game continued in your mind. Many people find themselves miserable, living for *someday*, assigning power and happiness to a delusional circumstance cast far into the future. As a result, so many grow disenchanted with life, lost in a reality where our projected fantasy is always out of reach.

How often have you told yourself that someday you will enjoy life when x, y, or z happens? Or, stated that you will be happy *someday* when you realize your dreams? Have you said that someday you will take that trip? Or someday you will start working out? What about when you say that once you make enough money, then you will do what you really want to do? Or better yet, you got that job you always wanted, you got the house, you got the car, you are in the perfect relationship, you moved to the town of your dreams, only to realize you were still not happy or still did not feel peace within. Let me share a little secret with you. There is only one thing standing in the way of you being happy today: *Your Perception*. There is only one thing holding you back from having peace within: *YOU*. There is no power in living for *someday*. Your power is in the NOW!

Peace and happiness are a state of mind. If you want to manifest a specific state of being, reality, or abundance in the physical realm, you must embody that which it takes to live that dream right now. Happiness is found in the journey, not the destination. The greatest dancers to ever live danced every day because they loved to dance, not because they attached to some outcome of their dancing. The greatest actors to ever live acted every day because they loved to act, not because they attached to some outcome. The most successful entrepreneurs live for the deal, not for the riches that follow.

Most successful people do not attach their success to the future; they base it on how far they have come. Oprah Winfrey did not start with her own talk show; she started one day at a time, one job at a time because she loved her craft. Our famous athletes did not start as professional athletes; they began one team and one practice at a time. The greatest Spiritual Leaders did not start as icons; they began one prayer at a time. The most famous composers did not start by writing symphonies; they began one note at a time. They chose to live their dreams one day at a time. They all had to master the art of embodying their dreams each day. They took advantage of the *Law of Attraction*, by seeking and being their *Truth* to manifest their dreams in the present moment.

Someday does not exist. All we have is today. Every day for the rest of your life will be another version of today. You disempower yourself by thinking that someday you will get to do what you truly desire to do. This is your life. It is not your dress rehearsal. Life is NOW!

Day 16 Practice

LIVE IN THE NOW

LAW OF GROWTH

Nothing in the Universe is still; everything is in motion and is designed for expansion. There is no time in the spiritual realm; however, in the physical realm some things take time: such things as growing a plant, becoming a dancer, or building a home. This Universal Law allows us to witness and measure our ability to manifest and demonstrate through the space and time continuum.

Today's practice is to **LIVE IN THE NOW!**

Where in life have you been living for 'someday'? Make lists of all the things that you think will make you happy *someday* as follows:

➢ Create a list of things that you thought would make you happy, but you never fully accomplished or were short-lived in bringing you happiness.

➢ Create a list of your dreams and the things you would like to accomplish.

➢ Create a list of the obstacles that are stopping you from the things you want to accomplish. For example, are you waiting for something to happen so you can live the life you want to live? Are you waiting to make enough money so that you can finally do what you really want to do? Are you waiting until you are the ideal weight to get back into the dating world? Are you waiting to get enough information to know what you want to do for a career? Are you waiting to write your book when you have enough courage? What are you waiting for? What are you putting off until someday?

The only thing standing between your dreams is your procrastination and your state of mind. Stop waiting!

Day 17

Judgment

You have the power to strip away many superfluous troubles located wholly in your judgment, and to possess a large room for yourself embracing in thought the whole cosmos.

~Marcus Aurelious

One day a couple came to me for spiritual counseling. I told them I wouldn't work with them together, but I would work with both individually. They annoyingly asked, "Why?" I said, "I simply don't counsel couples together; it never amounts to anything other than more arguments." They got a little more annoyed and started to make their case for me to work with them together asking, "How are we going to fix our problems separately, when our arguments are with one another?"

Wanting to make my point, I asked them, "What do you argue the most about as a couple?" They paused, looked at one another and then looked back at me with the same story. He said, "She is always telling me that I don't listen with enough compassion and that I'm constantly trying to tell her what to do. I feel like no matter what I do, I can never make her happy." She said," He is always trying to fix me instead of just being there for me. I feel like he doesn't understand me."

The moment you cast judgment on a person, place, or thing, you instantly set the human vicious cycle into motion. The instant you make another person wrong, they must turn that wrong onto you. Furthermore, the moment you judge yourself, you set into motion a whole stream of negative chemical reactions within. Judgments can be positive or negative, but regardless, when you judge, you set energy into motion. When you judge anything as negative, you instantaneously experience a negative feeling. When you judge anything as positive, you instantaneously experience a positive feeling. The entrapment of life is being the effect of your own creation. The secret to unlocking your own prison cell door is neutrality.

Let's continue to expand your *Consciousness*. You learn true wisdom through relative experiences, thus with this knowing, begin to embrace all aspects of life, understanding that the *Universe* wants to teach you neutrality and equanimity. Surrender to the ebb and flow and honor the parallel coincidences and paradoxes life offers. Expansion of your thoughts and perspective liberates you from all chains of suffering. When belief systems alter, you start to flow freely and naturally in this beautiful journey called life. There is nothing you cannot overcome or achieve. Recognize the enlightenment, not as a destination, but as the consummate of all experiences, delivering you to freedom. Every cell of your body, every star in the sky, every moment you experience has infinite wisdom, infinite possibility, and infinite opportunity to guide you in *Divine* connection, *Truth*, and happiness.

Marcus Radius Bracket was a famed Greek emperor who won the greatest battle of all: the battle within. He left a legacy behind his famous victories in gruesome physical massacres and powerful battle wars, but most importantly, he left a legacy rooted in his character. He is remembered as the philosopher king who had a strikingly blameless and wonderfully temperate way. In his work *Meditations*, he describes how to find and preserve equanimity amid conflict by following nature as a source of guidance and inspiration. He was one of the first leaders known to man who spoke of a collective approach to *Consciousness* and specified how important discipline and focus are, as well as the active pursuit of being a good person.

It was his ability to analyze the judgment he had of himself and others, which inspired his epiphanies based on a cosmic perspective, developing his cognitions about the *Universe* and life itself. I cannot imagine what it would be like to live in the gladiator days, so far removed from our first world problems and luxuries of living in the technological age; however, that is not to undermine the bloodshed of the heart that so many of us experience today living in the modern world. I believe, without a doubt, that many people experience life from a place of torture; incarcerating themselves through self-inflicted judgment. It is my belief that most of mankind would greatly benefit from this famous man's cognitions; that the progression of humanity is in fact dependent upon our learning how to master neutrality and equanimity.

THE MOMENT YOU ASSIGN A POSITIVE OR NEGATIVE MEANING TO ANYTHING, YOU INSTANTANEOUSLY EXPERIENCE A POSITIVE OR NEGATIVE FEELING

Your mind is the most powerful weapon you have; however, within the great internal battlefield, there are only two opponents: you and yourself. You can instantaneously create heaven or hell at the speed of one single thought. The moment you judge anything, you instantaneously experience a positive or negative feeling within yourself, which in turn, starts to bring you more and more thoughts similar in nature. It does not matter if you are judging someone else or yourself; regardless, you experience the effects of your creative thought. The extent to which you place a positive or negative meaning and assign a value accordingly, your experience is exaggerated in direct proportion. Thought affects experience.

Day 17 Practice

STAY NEUTRAL

LAW OF RHYTHM

Life is an energetic flow of vibration that moves in a cyclical manner; day becomes night, tides rise and fall, the heart beats in and out. This law brings balance and order through its centering equilibrium. Extreme beliefs, judgments, and intense actions, are brought to neutral through the process of this law. Industrial markets are corrected via this symmetric axiom swing.

Today's practice is to **STAY NEUTRAL!**

➢ To become cause over life, one must be able to avoid reacting to it. Practice taking a breath between stimulus and your response.

➢ There is great power of choice in that sacred moment. Practicing staying neutral is the key.

➢ Instead of immediately assigning a positive or negative meaning to what does or does not occur today, breathe and then decide what you wish to create. The rhythm of life can be mastered by you when you stay neutral.

Day 18

Victimhood

*I am so lucky and blessed for all the wonderful things that I do have.
Life is too short to think about all the things you don't have.*

~Jaycee Lee Dugard

On June 10, 1991, Jaycee Lee Dugard was kidnapped from her bus stop on her way to school. That day, media trucks, police with dogs, and investigators interviewing neighbors, monopolized the block. Everything was on lock down. They shut down the streets surrounding the community and the entire town was glued to the television hoping for the report that she had been found. A day went by with no sign of Jaycee. After a week, everyone tied pink ribbons all over the trees throughout the community. Those ribbons continued to hang week after week as a blinding reminder of devastation and pain. When a child disappears, the worst is automatically feared. Authorities say that if a child is not found within 72 hours, then the chances of finding the child are slim.

I remember the event like it was yesterday because I was staying at my mom's house that summer, and her home was less than two blocks away. Every day, I drove by Jaycee's home as I came and left from the main street. The pink ribbons stayed hanging on those trees that entire summer and were still there every year that I came back to visit my mother. My heart would drop just thinking about her family never having closure; never knowing what happened to their only daughter.

Eighteen years later, a miracle happened. News channels across the world broadcast live on television with a resounding shock and joy that Jaycee Lee Dugard had been found. I was personally overcome with joy and relief, with tears welling up in my eyes, and a heartfelt lump in my throat. I sat down and clutched my knees, "Oh my God! How is it possible?" Eighteen years later, this is a true, and much needed miracle. She had hidden for 18 years in the backyard of a kidnapper, held captive, raped, and tortured. She bore two of his children without any medical help or hospitalization. Her story is incredible, but the true miracle lies in her ability to rise above and persevere. Instead of focusing on her victimization, she prevails in reclaiming her life. Her survival instinct is inspirational and profound. Since being found, she has written a book, married, and continues to be the voice of the miracle of the human spirit and an inspiration to us all.

The mind has the ultimate power to create, innovate, and thrive no matter the circumstance. You always have the election to focus on what is wrong or what is right. You always have the choice to hold onto resentments or forgive, moving onwards and upwards. This does not mean you do not hold people accountable or should stay in dysfunctional situations, but through this process, you release the angst and suffering within. You realize that the only thing that can keep you suffering after an event has occurred is your own mind. You always have the choice of what you energize, re-creating yourself as the victim or focusing on creating a life you love.

When you stay in victimhood, you are mentally assigning something outside of yourself as being more powerful than your *Consciousness*. The degree to which you place power outside of yourself is the degree to which you become powerless. Reclaiming your power and your life is the path to empowerment. It is your birthright to have emancipation from suffering.

Viktor E. Frankl's (2006) *Man's Search for Meaning,* is a book of memoirs of his experience as a psychiatrist laboring through four Nazi death camps. He notes how the only survivors from these devastating death camps are people who found a reason to live and meaning for life despite their circumstances. He states that man cannot avoid suffering; however, he can choose how to cope with it, find individual meaning, and learn to move forward. It is a remarkable book displaying resolute conviction discussing how the primary human drive is not for pleasure but the pursuit of what we find meaningful. Frankl rightly observes that fulfillment is defined as the significance in the very act of living.

Spiritual work offers a miracle shift of perception, delivering us to gratitude for the pain and suffering we have gone through. It becomes the driving force helping us to connect and commit to making a difference. Suffering often becomes the impetus for desiring to live, breath, and love. How you choose to overcome it determines who you are as an individual and the effect you have on the world.

Day 18 Practice

FORGIVE AND SET YOURSELF FREE

LAW OF TRANSMUTATION

This is the metamorphosis of the ethereal realm into physical reality. Energy is condensed and formed via the mind, so what is held in Consciousness must transform into material form. This is the perpetual process because energy is infinite in its expansion. What the mind focuses on informs the creative medium of the Universe into action. Energy is incapable of being destroyed; therefore, it will take form. Thus, it is imperative to focus on what you want to manifest.

Today's practice is to **FORGIVE AND SET YOURSELF FREE!**

In knowing that your mental focus must transmute into form, it is important to let go of all victim mentality, sadness, and regret. Otherwise, you will inform the *Universe* of your negativity. Forgiveness is a must when it comes to unlocking the GODDESS and GURU within.

Take ten minutes to journal:

➢ What events and experiences do you still suffer from?

➢ Who do you need to forgive?

➢ Do you need to forgive yourself?

➢ What do you think it would take for you to make peace with your past?

➢ Are you ready to focus on what you want to create in your life and let go of regret, sadness, and past events?

➢ Use meditation as a key tool to begin to help you let go, release, and forgive.

Day 19

Perfectionism

The challenge is not to be perfect... it is to be whole.

~ *Jane Fonda*

Lights, camera, action! We have all been mesmerized. Our minds have been flooded with visual impressions our entire lives. Power, magnitude, wealth, glitz and glamour, morphed special effects, and photo-shopped filtered images have been fed to our brains and senses daily through social media, television, the silver screen, media, publications, magazines, and the press. Images have dazzled us all, manipulating our value systems and altering our priorities. They have ingrained idea after idea, thought after thought, which have turned into belief systems that have the potential to create feelings of inadequacy, as we try to live up to the expectations and idea of perfectionism that is constantly fed to us. It is time to lift the veil. Are you tired and sick of leaders attempting to show themselves in the light of perfection? An ideal they can never achieve because the dark side will always rear its head in the ugliest of ways at the timeliest moments. You are a perfectly imperfect, *Divine* individual, so isn't it time you started to live your live accordingly? In today's world, your soul is starving for transparency, authenticity and *Truth*.

How many of you have purged over glossy magazines and celebrity images enthralled by the magic of their beauty? Our culture is obsessed with Victoria Secret models and the style of the rich and famous, consistently delivering an unrealistic and digitally mastered perception of reality. The unattainable goal of perfectionism remains a toxic seed planted into your *Consciousness*, poisoning your joy and life experience.

The first step in detoxifying and cleansing the body of perfectionism is acceptance of the self. You can begin this process by focusing on the beautiful aspects of your physical body. When you focus on negative aspects, you create physical and mental stress. When you are stressed, your body secretes excessive levels of cortisol, which then increase fat storage (Talbott, 2007). Stress literally creates more fat, taking you further and further away from those glossy magazine ideals. It is a vicious cycle that can only be broken by a diet based on self-love and acceptance.

Take a moment and consider the implications and negative effects of the perfectionist ideal. Resistance is anything that is standing in the way of you fulfilling your dreams and living your *Truth*. It is the voice in your head telling you why you do not feel like doing something, the excuses, the justifications, and the thoughts that hold you back from demonstrating your dreams. Resistance often comes in the form of not doing anything, such as letting life happen to you rather than acting, or waiting for a perfect moment that never comes. Resistance is that cloud that stands between you and the sunlight.

Steven Pressfield's (2012), *The War of Art*, looks at the different forms in which resistance can belittle us. Pressfield focuses on the voice that keeps and prevents you from uniting with others, isolating you with feelings of unworthiness. What gets in the way of one area of your life also holds you back in all other areas. To be a fully expressive artist and creator, you must release yourself from the mental cage of invisible cultural binds, limited belief systems, thoughts of scarcity, and false identities. The path of least resistance is no resistance, for what we resist persists. Liberate yourself from feeling that you must be perfect and allow the beauty and joy in the imperfection.

I too, always thought that one day, after I had completed my spiritual work, that I would be perfect. I am proud to say, I am not perfect. I still have character flaws, only now I take responsibility for them. I still have negative reactions, only they are more infrequent and I view them as an opportunity for growth. You do not have to be a Zen master sitting atop the highest mountain in deep meditation. While it may be extremely difficult to completely disengage from the vicious human cycle, you can look within yourself, and make different choices regardless of where you are in life.

Mind chatter is that little voice that is always chiming in, always critiquing, analyzing, evaluating, and ranting. If you are thinking, "what voice?" That's it. It is the exact one that just asked the question. It keeps you from fully experiencing life, never allowing you to be in the moment, always filtering your experiences. It chimes in to tell you what is good and what is bad, judging and justifying. It tries everything in its power to convince you that we are separate and different, not smart enough or smarter than, superior or inferior. It is your internal editor that constantly points out all of your perceived limitations.

It is the inner dialogue that loves a good pity party and drunkenly stumbles through your perceived stories of abandonment and heartache. It is the true victim inside that speaks from the pain of the past and all the anxiety of your future. It is the bad friend within that will tell you exactly what you want to hear to confirm your limitations. It is your enemy dressed up as your best friend, the devil that rules carnage inside your head. It will agree with all your drama, trauma, and excuses. It will make the entire world wrong to make you believe otherwise. This mind chatter is standing in the way of manifesting your dreams. It disempowers you from taking full responsibility for connecting with others in your life. Mind chatter is the voice of ego, keeping you less than or better than, chaining you in captivity by tricking you into having a superiority complex, separated by your own grandeur. Mind chatter is the ego's game of winning, of separation, and survival. When the ego wins, you never get what you truly desire, which is love, connection, and authentic expression. If you identify with this self-sabotaging judge and jury, you will never live a life of abundance.

Buddhism describes the human mind as being filled with drunken monkeys, jumping around, screeching, chattering, and carrying on endlessly. Every single one of us has the mind of a drunken monkey; one that is clamoring for attention. Whether you think you can, or whether you think you cannot, you are right.

Truth was, is, and shall remain the voice of authenticity; the all-knowing intuition that resides within your heart, connected to all of life. It is the part of you that is committed to the fulfillment of your dreams. It is that part that conquers your deepest fears and allows for vulnerability and unconditional love. It is the voice that beckons you to fight for love, even when it seems like the entire world is against you. It sees the strength and beauty in all things. The voice calls your name when you are down on your knees begging for help, guiding and delivering you to a path of grace, honor, and prosperity. It also helps you to remember who you are, reminding you of what you need to do to live fully and without regrets. It demands you to live in your *Truth*.

Thinking and reacting from your monkey brain leaves you living in fear and anxiety about the future, and regret and shame from the past. Your mind gets weak and your body gets tired from the energetic drain it plays on your cells. *Spirit* is constantly communicating through your body, delivering positive or negative symptoms from the medium of your mind. When you stop identifying with the chatter of the mind and start to simply witness your thoughts, you free up the abundant energy within. Look for the connection that leads you forward and follow your intuition.

Day 19 Practice

LIBERATE YOURSELF FROM PERFECTIONISM

LAW OF NON-ATTACHMENT

This Universal Law is set into motion the moment you attach a positive or negative meaning to something that occurs or doesn't occur, which is the belief that the physical realm is more powerful than the creative power within. To have anything in life, you must free yourself mentally from attachment to it. Nothing in the physical realm is permanent and is only the mental equivalent of what is going on within Consciousness. Becoming neutral and equanimous is the key to directing this law.

Today's practice is to **LIBERATE YOURSELF FROM PERFECTIONISM!**

Find a quiet a space and reflect on your day:

➤ Notice how you are withholding your perfectly imperfect expression from the world.

➤ First, start to become conscious of all the ways you stop yourself from moving forward with you dreams because you feel you need to be perfect first.

➤ Finally, let yourself give your heart to the world through your individual expression and art, allowing your soothing voice to reign strong, taking over the belittling self-doubt voice.

> Are you ready to focus on what you want to create in your life and let go of regret, sadness, and past events?

> Use meditation as a key tool to begin to help you let go, release, and forgive.

It is time to paint your heart on the canvas of the *Universe*. You are beautiful and unique in your individuality and *Divine* imperfection, that makes you *"you"* and that is what the *Universe* needs, wants, and loves.

Day 20

Outlining & Controlling

The only willpower used in the process—if it could be called willpower—is a determination to keep the thought clear, to think about what ought to happen rather than about what ought to not happen, to be actively aware of harmony rather than discord, to believe that good will always overcome evil as light dissipates darkness.

~Ernest Holmes

It was an unusually rainy day when I sat down with a client to discuss why she was not fully thriving. I asked her what was going on in her life. She said she had just moved back to California, completely inspired and in love with Southern California beaches, but was having a difficult time getting her real estate business back up and running. She felt stuck in her career and kept trying to brain-storm innovative ways of advancing her business. She had been in real estate for about fourteen years and had seen incredibly abundant years. At one point, she had created a wonderful lifestyle selling real estate and traveling all over the world. She knew the market was not as hot as it was years back, but it had rebounded from the downturn, so she was stumped by the lack of results.

She identified herself with her career, linking her self-worth to what she was producing or failing to produce. As her career lacked to flourish, her self-esteem gradually lowered. She concluded that she must be the root of the problem and that something must be wrong with her. She believed that if she just worked harder or just networked better, then success in her career would follow.

So, I posed the question: "If money was of no object and you could spend your days doing what you truly desired, would you practice real estate?" She surprised herself when she said "no" and let out a deep sigh. There we sat, with a long and infinitely important pause. The dawn of a new era had begun as I witnessed her *Awakening*.

I invited her to take on the potential of a new viewpoint to her life situation. We explored the concept of an abundant *Universe* at all points in time. Sometimes when you feel lack, it is your inner guidance nudging you to move in another direction. Just as I was talking about this, I saw the sparkle in her eye and she said, "This is the third time someone has said this to me." She stated, "There have been a few people now that have planted the seed that maybe it is time for me to let go of the industry of real estate." She then indicated that she had heard that if something is said to you three times in a row, that it means the *Universe* is trying to communicate to you. She stated, "I've always wanted to do something in the spiritual and recovery world." For the next hour, we discussed possibilities of starting a business that runs Spiritual and Recovery Retreats in Southern California. The beautiful beaches that inspired her were still a triggering force and she propelled on to a new journey that took her on a route away from the problem.

Often people think that something is wrong with them. They think if they just change themselves within their relationship, career, or life, then it will work out. You simply need to change your thinking. When you get into flow with the *Universe,* abundance follows.

The Western culture is obsessed with production, getting rich, and climbing the social status ladder. Sometimes we get so narrow minded in our thinking that we close ourselves off to the opportunities of the world. We wrap ourselves in a box and see the world through gray lenses. We begin to feel like everywhere we turn, the doors are closed right in front of us. We keep banging our heads against the wall, thinking that if we just work harder, faster, and longer, then we will persevere. One of the fundamental Spiritual Principles and Universal *Truth*s is that life is ABUNDANT. You either allow this abundance or block it with your mind.

Often, you get what you want, only to find yourself more miserable and more unfulfilled than ever. Others have shifted their values, aligning with their souls' desires, yet still trying to force *how* things will manifest. This is called outlining, which is trying to control *how* a vision, dream, or calling is supposed to show up. You often try to manifest in specifics, with certain individuals, and in a certain way. When you do this, you are not allowing the abundance of the *Universe* to unfold for you. Instead, you create your own roadblocks, detours, and restrictive limitations that will hold you back and separate you from the realization of your individual *Truth.* Through acknowledging and working with *Universal Laws,* you can stop outlining and trying to control how your visions manifest in your life. When you empty your *Consciousness* of all thoughts delineating how things should show up, then you allow abundance to flow into your life. Open your eyes, mind, and heart to infinite possibilities and the pure potentiality that you are.

Day 20 Practice

GET IN THE FLOW

LAW OF ALLOWING

Life is a flow of energy exchange. What you resist persists. The moment you perceive something as negative that has or has not occurred, you instantaneously experience a negative feeling. This is the Universe's way of ebbing you towards the things that bring you joy. This law is designed for you to get into the current of life that aligns with your Truth and float down the river of ecstasy. The areas of life where you experience compulsion or dysfunction are ways that the Universe ebbs you towards your unique divine path that is specific to you.

Today's practice is to **GET IN THE FLOW!**

➤ Where in life are you experiencing resistance?

➤ Where do you feel stopped or powerless?

➤ What limiting beliefs do you have in that/those areas?

➤ What control are you willing to release to allow flow?

Step III:

ALIGN

Wealth & Wisdom

Day 21

Money: A Symbol of Your Consciousness

Wealth is the ability to fully experience life.

~Henry David Thoreau

I was contacted by a professional from one of the leading firms in Los Angeles: A young, attractive man with an incredible personality, well-known, respected, and at the top tier of his industry. A man on the cover of magazines and at the center of the media where many only dream of being. He was the perfect textbook model for the definition of success. Little would you know that he spent many sleepless nights and time on end battling with anxiety, and recounting stories of broken dreams and wasted opportunities. He felt trapped in his self-created prison cell.

He came to me because he felt miserable and was sick and tired of suffering from a deep-rooted internal pressure, self-judgment, and the frequent dialogue in his head that he was not good enough and would never produce enough fortune. He was a prisoner to the balance in his bank account, feeling as if he were drowning, and battling an insecurity that he would not have enough to pay for his family and worldly responsibilities. He was held by a high standard and faced strong pressure to be a provider for many, increasing his angst and feelings of inferiority. We looked at his belief system surrounding money and deciphered the correlation between his constant feeling of *not being enough* and *not having enough*. The epiphany was quick and clear; his belief system surrounding scarcity was the driving force for his success in business, but it was also the obstacle in reaching his full potential. He fell into the vicious cycle of the overwhelming feeling that he was not producing enough. Simultaneously, he engaged in the core self-destructive behavior that was preventing him from doing what he truly desired, while seeking peace of mind and abundance of wealth. He was so obsessed with making money, he focused on the feeling of not having enough, and he sent a message to the *Universe* of scarcity and angst, bringing back more of what he did not want. It was his obsession with trying to obtain money that was not allowing him to have it.

We dove even deeper and dismantled his thoughts around money to identify the root of his beliefs. Early in life, he was indoctrinated to believe that money is hard to get; that you must fight to keep it, and that money is scarce. In fact, he realized that he believed people have to kill for money. In one of our sessions, it dawned on him that, while growing up in South America, he had witnessed someone being murdered over money when he was a young boy. In that moment, he realized he no longer had to fight for money. He was free. I received a thank you letter a few months later with him raving about enjoying life without stress or anxiety, and stating that he had been able to save more money than ever before. But what struck me the most was not the sum of money he had accumulated since his profound epiphany, but the recognition of his love for life. That is true prosperity.

YOU ARE NOT HERE TO WIN THE RAT RACE OF MATERIALISM, YOU ARE HERE TO EXPERIENCE THE DEPTHS OF YOUR SOUL IN FORM

Money is just another form of communication in this world, whereas affluence is a way of being; a mindset that is based on relationships and co-creating. Your perception of money is based on the reflection of your relationship with yourself, your idea of self-worth, and of self-love. Do you believe you are worthy of abundance? Do you believe you are valuable?

The *Universe* reflects your beliefs regarding monetary wealth. In our culture, it is common to observe and to feel an imbalance in the realm of finance as it relates to the self. There are many multimillionaires who have not found the happiness they seek. We encounter people that are driven to accumulate massive wealth, yet feel insecure, envision scarcity, and fear that they will lose their money. Some hoard their money as they focus their energy into the belief that money is scarce. These internal dialogues and beliefs send a message of scarcity and fear to the *Universe*. Living out of fear, anxiety, a pressure to produce money, or need for status, all tells the *Universe* to bring us more of what we do not want. When you live in anxiety due to faulty thinking, then you are sending the message to the *Universe* that you are not enough.

I'm here to tell you, you absolutely are enough. You can constantly observe that it takes money to take care of yourself and the people whom you love; however, you must acknowledge the *Truth* that money does not equate to fulfillment, health, happiness, and love. Monetary wealth is important as it puts nutritious food on your table, a roof over your head, and it gives you the freedom to create astonishing experiences and own items that require the access to monetary wealth; however, all those things can be accomplished without actual cash. In fact, the concept that abundance is defined through monetary wealth stifles the creative process and impacts your ability to co-create. The key is to let go of the when and the how those things will come your way, and purely focus on your true wealth, which is defined by wisdom, knowledge, and relationships. The rest just falls into place.

MONEY IS SIMPLY A SYMBOL OF YOUR CONSCIOUSNESS

When you spend your time investing in developing your innovative capabilities and building relationships with people, you create authentic wealth. True wealth cannot be taken away from you; it comes straight from source, and it lives eternally inside of you. Your *Divine* nature is that of pure abundance, infinite progression, and everlasting co-creation. When you strip away your limited beliefs, you choose to live in your prosperity and abundance flows your way.

So how do you empty the *Consciousness* of limited beliefs surrounding monetary wealth? The first step as you *Awaken* is to identify your beliefs regarding money, wealth, abundance, and prosperity. What philosophies did your parents have about money? What values did you learn from your friends, from school, from society? What does money represent to you? What are your thoughts regarding wealthy individuals and those that are financially poor? Write down your responses and you will find that it is easy to elaborate and justify attitudes regarding monetary wealth. You will discover how simple it is to come up with detailed stories that support your philosophies regarding financial matters. Listen to yourself and try to identify the limitations in your belief system. You will quickly see how your limitations are keeping you from reaching your full potential and you will find yourself correcting your thoughts and expanding your *Consciousness*. Take the time to sit and understand your relationship with money and your clarity will multiply, allowing you to have clarity on what is holding you back.

An *Awakening* in the realm of wealth begins with awareness of your limited beliefs. Consider the implications of them on your life. Then, declare what you choose for yourself. Be specific in all you desire, but let go of any ideas of how requests are meant to manifest. Do you want a six-figure income? Envision it! But let go of the idea of how it is meant to come to you, trusting that the *Universe* will orchestrate the perfect set of events to turn your dreams into a reality. You may not know the when, you may not know the how: just let go, and trust that what you want is already yours for the taking. Set your intentions leaving the door open to infinite possibility.

What is your next step? Embody the mindset of gratitude and a helping attitude. Ask yourself how you can begin to serve others instead of focusing on your personal outcome. What skills and knowledge do you need to embody? When you begin to flow with the *Universe*, helping to bring others prosperity, you automatically redirect prosperity toward yourself. This is the magic of giving and receiving; the *Universe* doesn't know the difference. When we give to another, we activate the idea of prosperity as a *Collective Conscious*, telling the *Universe* to bring you more of the same, and in turn, gifts flow right back to you, while also enhancing the affluence of those that you have prospered. Prosperity is not defined by monetary wealth. You do not have to give gifts of monetary value to others. Value comes in all forms. A simple compliment, a helping hand, or assisting someone in reaching a goal. There are infinite ways to expand your *Consciousness* through abundance that will benefit society and in turn, help you attain your greatest desires.

Prosperity is the language of the *Universe*, a.k.a. *Divine* cash. It is distributed through people, coincidences, and paradoxical lessons. When you start flowing with the current of the *Universe*, you will see how things fall right in your hands through the assistance of others. The *Universe* devises and orchestrates the perfect plan so that you are at the right place, at the right time, with the right person. The *Universe* brings you what you need, from helping you learn a lesson to manifesting your desires. Prosperity is your authentic nature. When you step into grace, you become the channel for the *Divine*, bringing abundance to others at the most opportune times. A rich life is one of living a life that you love, and when you do, you naturally give back to the world.

Our culture is preoccupied with the production and identification of status through monetary gains. People can have all the wealth and fortune in the world, yet be broke in spirit and mind, miserable, and desperate trying to fill the never-ending abyss; an abyss that can never be filled by our material experience alone. One of the biggest myths we can believe in is that material gain equals fulfillment. Focusing on material fulfillment robs the energy and life of most our population, leaving us spiritually, mentally, and physically bankrupt. Money is merely an amplifier in your life. Wealth is not the key to your happiness; it is not the solution to all problems. The expansion of *Consciousness* is the gateway to all your life's desires. Your aim is to ignite your personal *Truth*. To be rich and radiate from within, to be opulent everywhere you go, to be the prosperity that the world needs and then watch as the abundance flows back to you in wealth and affluence.

Per Deepak Chopra (1993), the word affluence means to be flowing in the current of life. This currency is an energetic exchange of energy. It is a way of being, a mindset that is based on relationships and the ability to co-create. The *Law of Attraction* dictates that the secret to wealth is to embody that which you seek.

THE INSTANT YOU DECLARE MONEY MORE POWERFUL
THAN YOU, YOU BECOME DISEMPOWERED

A substantial portion of the population feels disempowered over the topic of money, believing and thinking that money is greater than them; an almighty and powerful force which has become idealized by the masses. When you give money this much power over you, you drift further and further away from its attainability. You begin to believe that your happiness is contingent on whether you have enough of it or not, living paycheck to paycheck, limiting your everyday activities, and ultimately, your dreams. Your balance in your bank account becomes the focus of your life, and you spend endless hours calculating numbers, feeling a sense of anxiety, a sense of self defeat, and a loss of control.

Day 21 Practice

CHOOSE ABUNDANCE

LAW OF ABUNDANCE OR SUPPLY

The spiritual Truth is that the Universe only knows abundance; the entire cosmos is designed with infinite elemental equations with unlimited combinations. This law is designed to have you align with absolute abundance. When you invert this law, or live in scarcity mentality, you will experience feeling bounded and fearful. The reality is, you have been endowed with a mind that is immeasurable in its ability to innovate and create possibilities. Even the material realm is lavish, and energy becomes unbounded through the incalculable synthesis of material particles. Your soul desires for you to awaken to your infinite potential and innovation. Let go of lack mentality. The Universe is ready to pour wealth unto you; open your arms and live abundantly!

Today's practice is to **CHOOSE ABUNDANCE!**

On a scale from 1-10 answer the following: (1= No, not at all & 10 = Yes, completely)

How disempowered do you feel in the realm of money?

1   2   3   4   5   6   7   8   9   10

How often does money dictate your ability to do things you want to do?

1   2   3   4   5   6   7   8   9   10

How much would your life change if you had more money?

1 2 3 4 5 6 7 8 9 10

*Results: Any score above 3 is a *Divine* sign to *Awaken to* the *Truth* of who you are!

➤ What limiting beliefs do you have about money? (Example: Only greedy people are rich. You must work hard for money. Money is the root of all evil).

➤ What limiting beliefs did your parents tell you about money through the words they spoke and their actions? (Example: Mothers don't work for money. Men are only valuable if they are the breadwinners).

➤ What does your culture tell you about money? What do movies tell you about money? What does the media tell you about money? What do your friends tell you about money? (Example: The limiting belief I learned by watching movies was that money brings happiness. Only rich men get beautiful women. I learned that it is normal to lie, cheat, and steal for money).

➤ List the times you handed your power over to money and decided money was more powerful than you. (Example: I remember the time I took a job that I hated because I was afraid I wouldn't be able to find a job I loved. I remember the time I dated someone because they had money and I didn't feel I could make enough money and be with someone I authentically cared about).

➤ If you had all the money in the world, what would you spend your time doing?

➤ If money was of no issue, who would you spend your time with?

➤ If you won the lottery today, what would you spend the money on?

➤ Now, ask yourself, "Why do I not believe in myself? What has me believing that I am not capable of creating my dream life without winning the lottery?"

➤ What is the impact and probable outcome of your life if you don't do your inner spiritual work to release limiting beliefs (Example: If I don't release these limiting beliefs I will live a life of lack and frustration. None of my dreams will come true and I will keep going around in circles, hoping for something to change outside myself)?

Day 22

Rich and Radiant: Law of Attraction

The power is from within, but we cannot receive it unless we give it.

~ Charles F. Haanel

On the day that William "Bud" Post III won a $16.2 million-lottery, it was said that he only had $2.46 in his bank account. William had lived a tough life. His mother passed away when he was just eight years old and his father sent him to an orphanage soon after. Before winning the lottery, he spent most of his life in miscellaneous jobs; cooking, driving trucks, painting, and working for traveling carnivals. In 1988, he finally got his break. Well, not exactly. It is also said that William went on a major shopping spree soon after winning the lottery. He purchased a liquor license, a lease for a restaurant, a used-car lot, and a twin-engine airplane. In a small amount of time he spent more than his annual distribution check of $395,000. Then he was almost killed when his brother hired a hit man in the pursuit of trying to claim his brother's winnings. Next, he was sued by his landlord/occasional girlfriend for one-third of his lottery winnings saying that he had pawned one of her rings for the money that he bought the winning lottery ticket with. The judge ruled in her favor. Long story short, he didn't comply and all his annual distributions were frozen, landing him in jail. He allegedly remarked, "I was much happier when I was broke."

According to the Certified Financial Planner Board of Standards, nearly a third of lottery winners declare bankruptcy. Studies have shown that within six months of winning the lottery, people generally revert to their previous lives (Adams, 2012). If they were happy, they return to being happy. If they struggled with depression, once the excitement of the win wore off, they would become depressed once again. If they struggled financially, they would encounter difficulties managing their wins and return to a lack of monetary wealth. Our richness is completely dependent on our *Consciousness*.

THE GREATEST PRODUCT TO PRODUCE IS THE HIGHEST VERSION OF YOURSELF

Money is not something that is out in the world or something to obtain. This is a delusional thought. If you were to study the financially wealthy, you would see that they do not hoard their money, rather, they are active investors. You must remember that financial wealth does not equate to fulfillment or success. There are many individuals that are financially wealthy, yet lonely and depressed, and confined and enslaved to the concept to their identity of maintaining their tangible riches. Truly *rich* individuals are wealthy because they have abundant lives. They benefit the people in their lives by the gift that they are to the world. Your only job is to always remember that you are *Divine*. This is the key to prosperity. Have you ever witnessed an individual who walks into a room full of vivacity and radiance? People gravitate to that individual who exudes a dazzling glow and a confidence that cannot be explained. It is these individuals who have expanded their *Consciousness*; they are highly in tune with themselves and have clarity and a direct path and understanding of their purpose. When you learn the ability to control your mindset, your actions align, and you become the person you are designed to be. You embark on a journey of success that directs you to your purpose and calling, and ultimately, the *Universe* delivers to you your heart's desires. Investing in yourself has the greatest return on investment.

Below are the mindsets of those who are living in abundance versus those living confined by their limiting beliefs. As you read through them, think about which mindsets you need to further develop to create abundance in your life.

Purpose vs. Confused

People with a wealthy mindset have intention and reason (their "why") that drives them toward success. This purpose is a core value that is aligned with their heart, mind, and soul. Therefore, it drives them when challenged in life. Purpose-driven people have true abundance (not just material, but a fulfilled life of prosperity) because they have aligned their authentic calling with bringing value to the world. People with a confused mindset send mixed messages to the *Universe* and therefore get mixed circumstances back. Often, they believe they want something, only to get it and then realize it will never bring them joy. Confused people have a challenging time having a prosperous life because they look to the world for their happiness when it can only be found within.

Commitment vs. Trying

People with a wealthy mindset direct specific energy upon universal mind with total conviction. They have decided to be successful. It doesn't matter if they know "how" they are going to accomplish their goals because they have faith and do not outline the process. Rather, they align with *Divine* right action and soar straight ahead. People with a scarcity mindset try to have success, but have a hard time winning because they have not decided at a core level to be successful due to limiting beliefs within their souls. Often, you will witness 'trying' people going around-and-around in circles, zigzagging, or starting and stopping projects. Life is chaotic and disorganized. They tend to justify why they aren't getting the results they desire out of life.

Leader vs. Victim

Leaders are powerful because they take 100% responsibility for their lives. Their wealthy mindset is all about directing energy, people, and circumstances towards success. They focus on their accomplishments instead of focusing on what they haven't accomplished, celebrating and giving positive reinforcement to their *Subconscious*. They tend to be idealists and see opportunities instead of obstacles. On the contrary, those with victim mindsets tend to blame people, circumstances, and the world for their failure. The victim mindset is passive and reactive to situations, markets, and the economy.

Now vs. Someday

Those with wealthy mindsets understand that the *Universe* only knows the present moment. They realize that their present actions determine their future results. Everything is acted upon, delegated, or scheduled the moment it comes across their desk, email, or phone. Those with a scarcity mindset believe they need to do xyz before they can begin. They tend to over-plan, over-analyze, and procrastinate.

Opportunities vs. Problems

Those with a wealthy mindset view all problems as opportunities. They see challenges as a game for growth. They shift hardship into lessons and transform pain into gain. The wealthy mindset understands how to tap into Universal Intelligence and innovation to solve any problem. Those with a scarcity mindset focus on why they can't accomplish things due to problems. They tend to draw in more problems because they are constantly informing Universal Law with fear, anxiety, and drama.

Creating vs. Reacting

People with a wealthy mindset tend to live life on their terms. They proactively demonstrate thriving relationships, systems, and platforms. The wealthy mindset realizes that creation has no bounds. Individuals with a scarcity mindset constantly react to life. Their internal navigation system is constantly being pushed around by the circumstances of their life. They tend to respond in a fight or flight manner.

Assets vs. Liabilities

Individuals with a wealthy mindset understand that they must be an asset to the world to live a life of abundance. They invest in people who help bring their life and business higher, thriving together. They invest in business assets that rise in value, compounding and proliferating. They focus their time on building products and services which are residual and bring everlasting prosperity. Those with a scarcity mindset invest in liabilities because they are liabilities themselves. They tend to draw people into their lives that bring little value. They invest in material belongings that depreciate, leaving them in debt.

Action vs. Analyzing

People with a wealthy mindset are actively in the game of life. They take extraordinary action, tweaking their performance as needed. They understand that life rewards initiative and gives critical feedback through the *Law of Cause and Effect*. They also realize that every little action and word they speak are powerful acts that inform life. Those with a scarcity mindset spend most their time analyzing and pondering. They are constantly trying to figure it out.

Productive vs. Inefficient

Productive people have a mindset that expresses the heart's specific message with the least amount of effort. To be efficient is to have the effect one desires. This mindset is organized, completes cycles, follows through, and simplifies its focus to one thing at a time. The opposite is true of those with a scarcity mindset, who often have difficulty completing cycles or following through with relationships (jobs don't get completed, projects go unfinished, relationships get severed or dwindle off, etc.) It also includes the inability to stop undesired actions, doing the same thing over and over without any real production, insanity, addiction, circular action, etc.

Leverage vs. Weakness

Individuals with wealthy mindsets understand how to exert less force upon life while getting greater results. They leverage relationships and resources to get the most out of life. They are proficient in risk management and create balanced success; however, those with a scarcity mindset stay small, thinking they can do it all on their own. They rarely take risks or take too much risk, gambling away their security.

Transcending vs. Transactional

People with a wealthy mindset focus on serving instead of selling. They realize that two minds have infinite potential. Furthermore, these transcending relationships often compound into large communities, tribes, and organizations. The transactional mind only thinks about what is in it for them. They take what they want and then eventually are left with a life destined for scarcity. They live in the daily 'to do' list instead of seeing the bigger picture.

Passive Income vs. Paycheck

Individuals with a wealthy mindset understand the power of their mind and their ability to infinitely create. They focus on building income that continuously generates even after the initial energy to generate it. Whereas, the scarcity mindset lives paycheck to paycheck, unable to break free from working by the hour in exchange for getting paid.

Quantum Leap vs. Linear

A prosperous mind thinks in leaps and bounds. They focus on what they are good at, and in doing so they exponentially become much more productive. They set extraordinary goals, which demand the mind to innovate. Also, they spend their time building the right relationships that will exponentially guarantee success; however, the linear thinker tends to try and do it all. Scarcity mindset believes it must do everything step-by-step and leaves them burnt out and having their confidence decrease.

Day 22 Practice

GIVE, SERVE, LOVE

LAW OF COMPENSATION

Life is an energy exchange; each person is compensated in a like manner to how they contribute. There is an identical correlation in the amount of value you give, to the value you receive. There is also an equal atonement to the expense of your action. This natural amending mechanism is the process of redemption, bringing balance and order. Example, you reap what you sow, you get back what you give.

Today's practice is to **GIVE, SERVE, AND LOVE!**

Whatever you seek in life, give it today.

- ➢ If you seek money, give money or help another rise in their prosperity.
- ➢ If you seek health, exert energy from the body and align with Mother Nature.
- ➢ If you seek love, give it without the need for it in return.
- ➢ Give a gift, a smile, or a compliment to a stranger.
- ➢ Give in service to a community or someone you know in need.

Day 23

Abundance and Prosperity: Your Birthright

People say that what we're all seeking is the meaning of life. I don't think that's what we're really seeking. I think what we're seeking is an experience of being alive.

~Joseph Campbell

I once ascended to the firmaments. I first went to see Hell and the sight was horrifying. Row after row of tables were laden with platters of sumptuous food, yet the people seated around the tables were pale and emaciated, moaning in hunger. As I came closer, I understood their predicament. Every person held a full spoon, but both arms were splinted with wooden slats so he could not bend either elbow to bring the food to his mouth. It broke my heart to hear the tortured groans of these poor people as they held their food so near but could not consume it.

Next I went to visit Heaven. I was surprised to see the same setting I had witnessed in Hell – row after row of long tables laden with food. But in contrast to Hell, the people here in Heaven were sitting contentedly talking with each other, obviously sated from their sumptuous meal. As I came closer, I was amazed to discover that here, too, each person had his arms splinted on wooden slats that prevented him from bending his elbows. How, then, did they manage to eat? As I watched, a man picked up his spoon and dug it into the dish before him. Then he stretched across the table and fed the person across from him! The recipient of this kindness thanked him and returned the favor by leaning across the table to feed his benefactor. I suddenly understood. Heaven and Hell offer the same circumstances and conditions. The critical difference is in the way the people treat each other. I ran back to Hell to share this solution with the poor souls trapped there. I whispered in the ear of one starving man, 'You do not have to go hungry. Use your spoon to feed your neighbor, and he will surely return the favor and feed you.' You expect me to feed the detestable man sitting across the table?' said the man angrily. 'I would rather starve than give him the pleasure of eating!' I then understood God's wisdom in choosing who is worthy to go to Heaven and who deserves to go to Hell ("Associates," n.d.).

Knowing that heaven and hell are right here, right now, in a state of *Consciousness*, then we can make the shift. As with every aspect of your life, *Spirit* desires love and connection. As we awaken and evolve, so does our wisdom and understanding of what it means to be wealthy. It is time for a change.

Per Paul H. Ray Ph.D. and Sherry Ruth Anderson (2001), in their book *The Cultural Creatives*, say there are over 50 million people in America who are tired of the emphasis in modern culture on the old paradigm of success. They indicate that there is an emergence over the last generation, with distinctive shifts in values and lifestyle that are changing the world. This group of people seek equality, spiritual and psychological development, well-being, innovation, love, and nature. They encourage investing into an education and care for the environment. They also see the grand importance of developing relationships and collaborating with one another.

Like all spiritual shifts, they are expanding their *Collective Consciousness*, looking beyond the self and turning within for the answers. They aim for ingenuity, eradicating the concept of time as linear, and thinking outside the box. They think of the *Spirit* as a community rather than an individual, creating camaraderie, synergy, and stepping up to a position of leadership.

True wealth begins by shifting into a broader *Consciousness*, moving past your tunneled vision, and into a state of creativity and innovation. As you expand your viewpoint, you develop a natural and innate desire to help everyone that crosses your path, envisioning and yearning for others to thrive and to find their ultimate happiness. For our culture to survive, we must progress into a *Collective Consciousness* of oneness and love.

In his famous book, *The Hero's Journey*, Joseph Campbell (2014) discusses that we all have a hero within. He indicates that the hero is a symbol of our ability to control a savage within us that is irrational. He describes The Hero's Journey as a life lived in self-discovery rather than a courageous act. The Star Wars series was based on Joseph Campbell's book. In the movie, Star Wars, Luke Skywalker finds the force within himself - the power of character to meet his destiny. He discovers that he can overcome evil and be set free. The ultimate objective of the quest is to seek and find the wisdom and the power to serve others. One of the distinctions that Joseph Campbell makes between the celebrity and the hero is that one lives only for the self while the other acts to redeem society. In seeking *Truth* and wisdom, you must look beyond the realms of illusion and regain your true self.

Day 23 Practice

GIVE YOURSELF FULLY TO LIFE

LAW OF CIRCULATION

All of life is an exchange of energy, a flow of giving and receiving. This is the current of Consciousness at an expanding rate, multiplied abundantly. Through this dynamic exchange, the Universe instantaneously responds to what you give to life. You reap what you sow.

Today's practice is to **GIVE YOURSELF FULLY TO LIFE!**

➢ There is only one explanation for your experience of lack of flow, or the feeling of being "stuck," and it is because you are not giving yourself to life.

➢ Where in life are you stingy?

➢ Where in life do you hold yourself back from giving your time, treasures, or talents to the world?

➢ How have you been suppressing yourself?

Love & Relationships

Day 24

Relationship Mastery: The Law of Love

Your task is not to seek for love, but merely to seek and find all the barriers within yourself that you have built against it.

~Rumi

The *Universe* is conspiring to bring you love. From the moment you wake, to the minute your *Consciousness* dozes off into a peaceful slumber at night, the *Universe* is at work. Acknowledge the hundreds of thousands of things that are conspiring for you. The sun shines despite a cloudy day bringing you life. The air you breathe has been billions of years in the making, which allows you the miracle to live on Earth. The trees live to give you oxygen, feeding your body with energy. The full moon comes time after time, influencing the tides so you can swim in the ocean's playground. The clouds separate, and sprinkle at dawn, for a beautiful glimpse of a rainbow that reminds you of this extraordinary experience. You can see how the challenges, obstacles, and problems are brought to you as an opportunity to learn, grow, and love. You experience a revelation regarding world events that once seemed evil and horrific, and view them as a wakeup call for all of humanity to come together in harmony. You shed tears of joy, knowing that if something does not feel right, you can act and change it.

THE PRIMARY RELATIONSHIP IS WITHIN; ALL OTHER RELATIONSHIPS ARE THE PROJECTION AND REFLECTION OF YOUR ABILITY OR INABILITY TO LOVE

First and foremost, the most important relationship is the one you have with yourself. All other relationships are the reflection of the primary relationship within. The inner work is to heal the connection between you to your Higher-Self. Every relationship that you encounter is the ultimate mirror that reflects the opportunity to create, grow and evolve. Relationships are the platform for learning and for your spiritual growth; a sacred space to observe your limited beliefs, your misconceptions, and your level of self-worth, by paying close attention to the people you are attracting, entangling with, and interacting with in your life. As you gain clarity and understanding of the deepest and purest desires within your heart, you no longer accept anything that does not align with that vision.

The most magical, mysterious, luminous, mystical concept of the *Universe* is love. It guides all life; it prevails, heals, surmounts the insurmountable, and makes the seemingly impossible, possible. We long for and seek it deep inside our hearts at the most profound level of the soul. It is that which births all creation and restores harmony. Love is an integral human guiding force, with power like no other. Love strips away everything that stands between you and it. Unveil your authentic nature, which is innately pure love. Tear down the walls, belief systems, and all which no longer serves you. Reduce the significance you place on relationships, and in doing so, free yourself from expectation and bask and marvel in the miracle of human connections. Dismantle all limitations of your mind's mythical concepts of love.

Our modern world breaks the old paradigms and stigmas of restricting love and relationships. The United States of America made history, legalizing same sex marriage on June 26, 2015; a giant leap toward equality and acknowledgement of the true value of love. Love transcends gender, age, and race, freeing you from your own self-imposed, restrictive, and judgmental rules about love and entitlement to it. Despite the technological advancements in the world and our combined *Universal* knowledge, as a species, we struggle immensely in the realm of relationships. There seems to be no rhyme or reason, no logic, and no book that has solved the world's relationship issues. Universally, mankind is still at war with itself over the definition, the importance, and the integrity of love. The time has come to look at your concepts and misperceptions about love so that you can release what no longer serves you and begin to create, from a blank canvas, a painting of a life full of love.

There are three levels of relationships: the ego demands to know, "what is in it for me?" The inter-related standpoint questions, "what is in it for us?" The synergic asks "what is in it for the *Highest Good*?" Letting go of traditional concepts of relationships further expands your *Consciousness* and releases you so that you can focus on the authentic lover within. Allowing your spiritual practice to flow freely into your relationships is the ultimate method to achieve further expansion of *Consciousness*, helping you to find your perfect match, which serves mankind and the *Universe* in ultimate fulfillment. We are all different and that individuality has a purpose. We all have a role in this world, and what serves one can greatly differ from individual to individual. It is not for you to judge, but merely to work on yourself and find your own self-expression.

When you fully embody the essence of who you want to attract, life unfolds instantaneously. It is the *Divine* law of the *Universe* to have that which you are. The *Law of Attraction* is the name given to the maxim "like attracts like," which in New Thought philosophy is used to sum up the idea that by focusing on positive or negative thoughts, a person brings positive or negative experiences into his or her life. In quantum physics, the *Law of Attraction* teaches us that thoughts become things; reiterating that your intentions, impulses, and your inner vibrational selves are continually attracting your circumstances, experiences, and furthermore, the evolution of the self, at large, mankind.

So, the work remains the same. It involves de-cluttering your life from chaos, miscommunications, and clearing it of anything that is not what you powerfully desire. You let go of all past relationships or people who are clearly not *The One* so that you can communicate to the *Universe* your commitment. You stop sending mixed messages to the *Universe* and stand in absolute clarity. If you desire, you learn how to hold a sacred space for *Divine* love to emerge and be received. First, you must become the love of your life, knowing that love only comes from the source within and radiates out, and reflects from *The One*.

Step 1: Wake up and discover who you are and how you relate to what does or does not occur within your relationships. (Examples: I am someone who gets upset when my partner is late for our dates; I am someone who enjoys being intimate.)

Decide and choose if you wish to continue being who you are in your relationship. (Examples: I do not wish to be someone who keeps getting upset when someone shows up late; I do wish to be someone who enjoys intimacy).

Step 2: Reprogram your thinking and ways of being through meditation, expanding *Consciousness*, affirmations, visioning, intuition, and mindfulness. Command your *Subconscious* and the subjective mind, and *Universal Law* with the conviction of your heart.

Step 3: Align with the *Truth* of who you are and the laws of the *Universe* as you practice being authentic and transparent, while staying in harmony and peace. Follow your bliss.

Step 4: Affirm by creating your Life's Purpose Statement and your Daily Spiritual Practice. Live your *Truth*!

Day 24 Practice

LOVE WITHOUT LIMITS

LAW OF LOVE

Love informs creation and the law is the internal mechanism of life that guides all things to order, harmony, and love. If the creative process is inverted to create chaos, harm, or disorder, this law will bound its effects. Love is the expression and expansion of Spirit (Your Higher-Self) through desire in terms of creation, through you as you. All of life is designed to awaken the Self to greater love.

Today's practice is to **LOVE WITHOUT LIMITS!**

On a scale from 1-10 answer the following: (1= No, not at all & 10 = Yes, completely)

To what extent do you feel unconditional love for yourself?
1   2   3   4   5   6   7   8   9   10

Do you embody that which you seek?
1   2   3   4   5   6   7   8   9   10

Do you stay open and minimize the projection of your fears and limiting beliefs into your relationships?
1   2   3   4   5   6   7   8   9   10

*Results: Any score below 30 is a *Divine* sign to your *Awakening* to the *Truth* of who you are!

➢ What limiting beliefs do you have about relationships (business and romantic)? (Examples: love hurts; people don't care; relationships never last).

➢ What limiting beliefs did your parents instill in you regarding relationships through the words they spoke and their actions? (Examples: people are self-centered; committed relationships are passionless; nobody stays together).

➢ What did culture and society teach you about love and relationships? What did the movies tell you about love and relationships? What did the media tell you about love and relationships? What did your friends tell you about intimacy (Examples: people live happily ever after; relationships are dramatic, dysfunctional, and emotional)?

➢ List the times you based your self-worth on your relationship (Example: I am not enough; I need validation from others to feel good).

Relationships are the opportunity to discover who you are and how you relate to what does or does not happen in life. They are here to assist in strengthening your responsibility.

Take ten minutes to journal:

➤ What things do you like within relationships?

➤ What do you not like within relationships?

➤ What expectations do you have around relationships?

➤ What limiting beliefs do you have that you are willing to give up to experience more freedom in your relationships?

Day 25

The One: You Are the One You've Been Waiting For

Life doesn't give you the people you want; it gives you the people you need...to love you, to hate you, to make you, to break you, and to make you the person you were meant to be.

~Walt Whitman

Before *Awakening,* I was completely co-dependent in my relationships. When things were good in my relationships, I was flying high. When things were going poorly in my relationships, I was feeling down. My life was a never ending roller-coaster of ups and downs, highs and lows, breakups and makeups. For most of my life, I was waiting for *The One.* I had bought into the fairytale story I had watched in movies, the one where the man rides up on his white horse and we live happily ever after. I thought a relationship was going to complete me. I had assigned relationships as my Higher-Power. It was a terrible way to live, leading me down a path of self-destructive patterns. Finally, I created my low, where I found myself in a completely dysfunctional relationship. Just the thing I needed to wake up, demanding me to learn self-love and bring me to the *Truth* that my Higher-Power is within. The reality is that I couldn't be in a loving relationship until I learned to love myself.

The primary relationship is within you; all other relationships are the projection and reflection of your ability or inability to love. The relationship between the individual self and the Higher-Self is the core relationship. It is the ultimate yoga, the merging of the individual mind with the highest *Consciousness* in unity. If you awaken to the metaphysical reality that relationships are the out-picturing of your *Consciousness*, you can begin to use love as the grand teacher in life. Love is the ultimate mirror of who you are, experiencing the union with all that is, through communication and acknowledgement. When you finally let go of everything that is holding you back from being loving, you naturally walk through life *making love to it*, giving love at some level everywhere you go; whether it be a smile, a friendship, a gesture. To love is to express your divinity. Love is eternal, it is ever-giving, and it comes from one source: *Within*.

THE ONE IS ALWAYS YOU

You are the one you've been searching for. In modern culture, it is customary practice to place the concept of *The One* outside of the self, believing that you need another to complete you, and that you cannot find true fulfillment without the missing part of the whole. Spiritual work shifts that limited concept from outside the self to within. *The One* has been with you all along, it is always, has always, and always will be, you that you are searching for. You are the amazing person that shines and radiates from the inside out when you love yourself. You hold sacred space for yourself, and in turn, hold sacred space for your beloved. Self-love is the key.

Being *The One*, you no longer seek external validation, nor any false identities, roles, or titles. You ask yourself, "What can I bring to life?" Instead of asking, "What can life bring to me?" There is no need to believe that anyone is right or wrong, because you know who you are. Becoming *The One* is taking full responsibility for the creating of your own experience, circumstances, and the expression of all relationships.

The One attracts the perfect expression of love and relationships. When you get in touch with that eternal aspect of yourself, you emit a magical glow. You learn to understand your infinite strength and wisdom. When you stand in this empowered space, chaos and deceit melt away from all circumstances. You become determined to live a radically extraordinary life. You know your birthright and become clear of your purpose and calling. You feel this *Truth* within every fiber of your soul, every cell of your body, and with the conviction of your heart. You become the pillar to everyone in your life solely by what you embody. You are the essence of love through the ability to take care of yourself, and love yourself, while loving others more profoundly.

Romance, partnership, friendship, marriage, and all relationships become fulfilling on all levels. You become liberated through self-expression and extraordinary communication. It is a transcending experience when you give and serve others, believing in their own potential. *Awakened* relationships become the platform for birthing all types of creativity to this world; a calling for a greater purpose. This could be art, children, or a company that is conscious and makes a difference.

Unique expressions of love exist for each of us, in our own authenticity. What is right for one individual may be completely different for another, and you must find your *Truth* and accept this notion. For example, some people chose to be clearly monogamous, while others love being single and dating multiple people. There are all types of diverse ways people love one another. What I desire is for you to live unbounded within your unique and individual *Truth*. Living authentically and transparently is the key to living powerfully and joyfully. Be that which you seek. The most important thing we can do to call in *The One* is to be *The One*! Be the equivalent of the type of person you seek. This is how the Law of Attraction works. You must ask yourself who you are in the realm of relationships.

Love is like electricity, flowing through you, and transmitted vibrationally from cell to cell. Love can give light, warmth, and energy if used constructively, or it can cause harm and pain. As you *Awaken*, you may come to realize that love works in the same way as all of life; as one gives, so do they receive. Love is the epitome of your cause and effect *Universe*. It is the law of giving and receiving, what you put out comes back. How it comes back, may not be from that exact person or circumstance, but it comes back in a symphonic karmic way. When you allow love to flow through you, it automatically reflects through the law, right back at you.

The shift in all life, including love is no longer looking to the outside world for change. You must first change yourself and be that which you seek before the external world will show up accordingly. You can no longer look to the outside world for love, happiness, or fulfillment; it must come from within. As you step into your *Awakening*, you begin to cherish your relationship as sacred playgrounds to express and share love. You see how one of the main purposes of relationships is to discover who you are and how you relate in relation to what does or does not occur. Once you discover and acknowledge the relativity of how you respond, you then have choice. Unbounded love becomes responsible.

Love is the only *Truth*, but just because you love someone does not mean that you can be in a relationship with that person. There are major distinctions between functioning and dysfunctional relationships. Being in a relationship involves workability, agreements, purpose, intentions, objectives, barriers, and freedoms.

According to Werner Erhard, an involvement is a relationship that excludes the world. He gave a brilliant talk on the distinction between love and relationships and explained that our awareness of how we relate to something or someone is our understanding of relationships. He said, "Relationships are an understanding and being aware of how we relate to something or someone. Whereas, involvement is to make intricate, entangled, or complicated, to draw or hold within itself." ("Werner," 2013). The ultimate question remains: Does your relationship contribute to the world? Love is a positive connection and deep reflection of your alignment with the *Universe*. It remains your ultimate *Truth*.

Do you desire someone who is not your equivalent? Do you desire someone who has an abundant mentality, but you are stingy and come from lack? Do you expect your partner to show up happy all the time, yet you spend your conversations with friends complaining and engaging in negative talk? Who are you being in life? What are your internal belief systems? Do you desire someone who is loyal, yet you are constantly dating multiple people?

Set Your Intention

Now pretend you have a blank canvas and conjure your perfect scene, your chosen incredible life with your perfect soulmate. Are you being the person you would want your partner to be? What do you need to work on within yourself? Who do you need to become to attract that person? Now search within and ask the *Universe* to help you envision the person you need to be to become *The One*. Find clarity and set the intention of what you want for you and your partner, and then hold that vision. Do not allow any limited beliefs, fears, or doubts to enter your mind. The true master of manifesting does not allow anything negative to enter his mind. He simply lets go of trying to control how his dream will manifest and lives on the faith of knowing it is done. Focus on embodying being the person you need to be, through expanding your *Consciousness* and allowing yourself to live fully. Love is your birthright. It is who you are. When you know who you are and step powerfully into loving yourself, you naturally call in unbounded and limitless love. Learn the *Truth* and you will be set free to a love beyond your wildest dreams.

Day 25 Practice

BE THAT WHICH YOU SEEK

LAW OF ATTRACTION

This Universal mechanism is best described by the axiom; you attract and repel that which you are. This law is the culmination of all the Universal Laws and describes how you manifest and demonstrate through physical embodiment. Life sets into motion by the magnetic frequency of your soul which is created from your beliefs, the actualization of who you are, and the actions you take.

Today's practice is to **BE THAT WHICH YOU SEEK!**

Take ten minutes to journal:

➤ Are you being that which you seek in your relationships?

➤ List all the qualities you desire in a partner, and then ask yourself if you have all those qualities?

➤ Who do you need to become to have the relationships you want?

➤ Are you being a mirror within your relationships? Are you reacting or are you confidently creating what you are committed to?

Day 26

Sexuality: What's Love Got to Do with It?

It's not true that I didn't have anything on. I had on the radio.

~Marilyn Monroe

Sex is another microcosm of the macrocosm of who you are in this life. Sex can either be a beautiful expression of who you are or it can be a dis-empowering realm that leaves you heartbroken, lost, and dysfunctional. Just like all areas of life, sex has many realms, experiences, levels, and perspectives. Like all spiritual work, the goal is to align the physical, mental, and spiritual, living your unique *Truth*. You may believe that the best sex is with someone you love on all levels, while others may have other preferences. You have heard of commitment, marriage, polygamy, monogamy, open marriage, gay, transsexual, heterosexual, and much more.

Sex is another gateway to observe how you are creating life. Is it a beautiful expression? Or is it an entangled entrapment? From a relative perspective, you may consider spiritual sex to be an experience in which there is expression from an authentic and genuine space, unifying hearts and souls; whereas objectifying sex, may be considered an experience in which people are viewed as objects and the soul feels separate. Discover the expression of your soul in the realm of sex. Like all things in this *Universe*, sex is another form of communication and it can be dynamically used to create something magnificent, or it can be used to create chaos and discord. You must be mindful of your actions, and the first step is to discover your desired form of expression within your love life. Learn to honor every person's *Truth*, as there are infinite ways of having sex and making love, just as there are people on this planet. There are also many spiritual practices that touch upon the topic of sex, such as Objectifying Sex, Tantra, and Kama Sutra; however, remember that there is not a single thing that is not spiritual in this life, only the perception that not everything is spiritual.

Oxytocin increases when we feel attracted to someone, which in turn stimulates dopamine to be released. While falling in love is at heart a reflection of our earnest desire, multiple factors can play into attraction, including your DNA, your senses, and the animalistic need for survival. The body exerts a response when romantic feelings are stirred; this includes flushed cheeks, racing heartbeats, clammy hands, and a general level of giddiness. Physically and chemically, the body alerts you to form an attachment to the object of desire, as chemicals that issue a sense of reward are released when being around that person. Lust is galvanized into action by the hormones testosterone and estrogen, stimulating your sex drive and libido. Attraction follows a deeper level of physical connection. Neurotransmitters called monoamines guide your physical responses and feelings. Norepinephrine, which is the chemical responsible for adrenalin, increases your level of sweat and your heart rate. Serotonin plays a vital factor in feeling "in love," as well as making you feel temporary insanity.

Love is no joke. It is one of the most important and powerful forces that moves in us, through us, and ultimately beyond us. Oxytocin is released in both sexes during an orgasm, creating an intimate bond. Oxytocin is the same chemical released during childbirth, and responsible for the bond between mother and child. Our physical bodies are naturally designed to promote our survival as a species (Borelli, 2014).

When you experience love and attraction, it is a sign that you are in alignment with your Higher-Self. What feels good is good. When you experience discord, or chaos, it is a sign you are imbalanced, or not being true to your inner self. All human beings can tap into this wondrous harmonic flow of life. Listen to what your body is telling you. Use your instinct and your emotions as your guidance system, as they are the most advanced system known to man.

The reality is that 75% of all women have never experienced an orgasm through sexual intercourse (James, 2009). Freudians would have us believe that a woman's inability to reach orgasm is because a woman has not grown up. Princess Marie Bonaparte, a woman closely linked to Freud, asserted that the optimum distance between the vagina and clitoris was 2.5cm, and that it was this measurement that was integral to achieving a female orgasm. She went as far as undergoing an experimental surgery to ascertain these measurements because of her own frigidity and difficulty achieving an orgasm (Moore, 2009).

The pressure on females to experience vaginal orgasms has been immense for centuries, stimulating an overwhelming sense of failure amongst women who have never experienced one. The modern woman is expected to be a professional, mother, a multi-tasker, but also a red-carpet walking, porn performer in the bedroom. Many women feel exhausted and not fulfilled. Why some women are fulfilled and some are not remains somewhat of a mystery. But understanding the limits women impose on themselves, and the rules women like to shroud in their lives through thought and learned stigma undeniably play a part in how free flowing and relaxed women allow their bodies to be.

Our entire culture is clearly experiencing disconnection from the soul, and more so in an intimate setting. People cannot seem to figure out why it feels like there is just something missing. The body can exhibit a wide array of symptoms, from low energy to full blown depression. For men, there seems to be a disconnect between having a strong sexual desire and wanting to be true to their hearts. They tend to feel guilt, shame, repression, and suppression. There is nothing more attractive than a man or woman who has gotten in touch with the eternal aspect within and stands firm in his or her *Truth*. The body is this dynamic instrument of sexual expression. The spiritual climax of life is to live in alignment with what the soul desires, which is love and connection, along with sexual fulfillment. May you transparently live your sexual *Truth*.

LOVE IS THE ONLY *TRUTH*

It is the most magical, mysterious, luminous, and mystical concept in the *Universe*. It is that which guides all of life; prevails, heals, and transforms the impossible into the possible. It is that which births all creation and restores harmony. We long for it, try and label it, place meanings on it, put it in a box, and hoard it. What we often do not do is cherish it, and allow ourselves to shower others with it and be showered by it. And, even more so, we do not allow ourselves to love ourselves. In fact, I would be so bold to say that until you truly love yourself unconditionally, with zero judgments and total admiration, that it is impossible to love another whole-heartedly.

The primary relationship of love is within you. All other relationships reflect your ability or inability to love. Love is the grand teacher in your life. Often you project your own conditional love, fears, and judgments onto others. It is the ultimate mirror of thyself, which reflects the union between communication and intimacy. The *Source* of love is always from within. Your job is to strip everything away that is standing between you and love. This is a process of unveiling your authentic nature, which is pure love. Tear down the walls, the belief systems, and all the *ways of being* that no longer allow you simply to love. This entails *Emptying the Consciousness* of the expectations, ideals, judgments, identities, and even the significances you place on relationships, so you can begin to experience the miracle that it is. When you withhold your love through conditional love, you are essentially denying your *Divinity*, and you annul the *Truth* within.

As Ernest Holmes stated, "So take a look at all the reasons you withhold, block, and deny love. Look at all your limited stories, judgments, and expectations that you are projecting onto the people in your life. Jot down all reasons you don't have the love you desire, and then look at them. Place that list into a box (just as that list has put you). It is that exact list that has kept your radiant heart suppressed and repressed from your *Divine* essence: *Love*! Love is the central flame of the *Universe*, the very fire itself. Love points the way and Law makes it possible."

Day 26 Practice

EXPRESS YOUR SEXUALITY

LAW OF GENDER

Within all creation is the masculine and feminine. The masculine is the aspect of manifesting that implants the seed of fertility. The feminine is the subjective womb of life that births the creation into form. Every thought is the masculine and every manifestation is the feminine. The form is the culmination of both. Energetically all things are held in perpetuity by Universal Consciousness. Sexuality is the Divine urge to create in its expression.

Today's practice is to **EXPRESS YOUR SEXUALITY!**

The first step in expressing your sexuality is discovering your *Consciousness*.

Make a list:

> ➤ What are the reasons you withhold, block, and deny your sexuality?

> ➤ What limited stories, judgments, and expectations are you projecting onto your sexual life?

> ➤ What are all the reasons you don't have the intimacy you desire?

Now, place that list into a box (just as that list has put you in a box). This list is that exact list that has kept you suppressed and repressed. Let it go!

Health & Wellness

Day 27

Symptoms: The Divine Signs

Illness does not come upon us out of the blue. They are developed from small daily sins against nature. When enough sins have accumulated, illness will suddenly appear.

~Hippocrates

One day, a client came in for a *Subconscious* session to address trauma. She had been raped a couple years back and it had really been affecting her ability to date. Prior to beginning the *Subconscious* part of the session, I asked her to explain a little about what had happened. She began to tell me about how she had been on a vacation, and talked about some of the backstory and circumstances around the incident. Suddenly, she stopped everything she was saying and just looked off in the air, as if in that moment, she had a great insight. Then, she looked at me, quivering in excitement, and said, "Oh my goodness, I just realized something. I have been having all these health problems ever since my rape. I put on 20 pounds, I have adrenal fatigue, I have a chest infection, and I even cut my eye. I just realized that avoiding the trauma of my rape has been making me sick!"

Often, when we think of disease, illness, or being sick, we think of viruses, bacteria, or infections. This is not always the case. In fact, most illness begins from one core factor: *Stress*. I invite you to take on the possibility that symptoms are the *Divine* signs from Spirit (your Higher-Self), communicating and guiding you toward your *Awakening*.

Let me ask you a question, if health is our most precious possession, why are we experiencing the highest rate of cancer, diabetes, obesity, stress, and depression our country has ever faced? What if I told you that you could live a life of vitality, longevity, and wellness? What if I told you that you have the potential of spontaneous healing from any dis-ease? What if I told you that the same energy that has created the bonds of your health is the exact energy that can free you to live a life of health?

My invitation to you is to let go of everything you have ever been told about the cause of dis-ease and illness and open your mind as we go on a journey of revealing ancient *Truth*s and wisdom about *Consciousness*. The mind is the source of ultimate longevity, wellness, and vitality.

Within each person is an infinite intelligence, an innate healer, and a life force capable of miracles. Whether you are dealing with the effects of aging or a major health issue, I would like you to consider that it all comes down to one thing: *Consciousness*. Physical and mental symptoms come from *Spirit*, our highest *Consciousness*, communicating that individually and culturally we are living out of harmony with Mother Nature and the Natural *Laws of the Universe*. Symptoms are the impetus for a *Divine* breakdown so that you *Awaken* and have a breakthrough. It is time to have a true healing, which can only be done through your *Awakening*.

When Hippocrates talks about sin, I believe he is talking about the simple *Law of Cause and Effect*, missing the mark of our true desires. Hippocrates was a brilliant man who revolutionized medicine in ancient Greece. He was the person who established medicine as a profession. At present date, every medical doctor that graduates from medical school takes the Hippocratic Oath. Unfortunately, it has been dramatically altered from the original doctrine.

Your body is born with intelligence that dates back for billions of years, if not to the beginning of creation. It has built-in systems that send off alarms of when you are creating health or when you are creating illness; you either feel good or you feel bad. Most illness is the side effect of stressful lifestyles and the toxic environments you have created. Dis-ease is the effect of creating a life of unease. Symptoms within the body, such as poor health, fatigue, backache, insomnia, anxiety, depression, diabetes, cancer, heart attacks and all illnesses, are the relative and inverted use of *Universal Energy*.

In 2009-2010, the National Health and Nutrition Examination Survey released some shocking statistics concerning overall health in adults and children. a) More than two in three adults have been found to be overweight or obese, b) More than one in three adults are obese, c) More than one in twenty adults are considered to have extreme obesity, d) About one-third of children and adolescents ages six to nineteen are overweight or obese, and e) More than one in six children and adolescents ages 6 to 19 are obese.

Obesity is a major health concern; it is common, serious, and costly. Other illnesses and grave causes for concern include anxiety, mental stress, and depression, which often go hand-in-hand with physical illness and all of these are on the increase across our society. Below are some additional statistics from the Journal of American Medicine (Ogden, Carroll, Kit, et. al., 2012).

More than one-third (34.9% or 78.6 million) of U.S. adults are obese. Obesity-related conditions include heart disease, stroke, type 2 diabetes and certain types of cancer, some of the leading causes of preventable death;

In the U.S., there was an estimated $147 billion in costs for treatment of obesity. Medical costs for people who were obese at the time, were $1,429 higher than those individuals of normal weight;

Anxiety disorders are the most common mental illness in the U.S., affecting 40 million adults in the United States age 18 and older (18% of U.S. population);

Depression affects approximately 14.8 million American adults, or about 6.7 percent of the U.S. population age 18 and older in a given year.

SYMPTOMS ARE DIVINE SIGNS FROM YOUR HIGHER-SELF TELLING YOU THAT YOU ARE NOT LIVING IN ALIGNMENT WITH YOUR *TRUTH*

Awakening begins with seeing the perfection of your health exactly as it is; perceiving any bodily symptoms as *Divine* Signs to align with Mother Nature and live a life of peace within. The truth is that you are an eternal spiritual being, immortal, and untouchable by any circumstance in life. You are not your body, you are *Divine.*

Day 27 Practice

LISTEN TO YOUR BODY

LAW OF PERFECT HEALTH

This Universal Law is the axiom that whatever is going on within your health is the mental equivalent of what is going on within Consciousness, individually and collectively. When we get out of alignment with Mother Nature and Universal Laws we experience ill-health. Within you is a born intelligence and an innate healer, capable of restoring harmony, well-being, and vibrant vitality. When the body is bogged down with toxins and negative emotions, it can't function properly. From a spiritual perspective, dis-ease is Spirit (your Higher-Self) communicating that individually and collectively we are out of harmony with life. Symptoms within the body, such as poor health and illness are the relative and inverted experience of our use of Universal Energy. From an absolute perspective, the Truth is that you are an eternal immortal spiritual being. You are not your body, you have a body. From a spiritual perspective, the only true disease is amnesia. However, if we choose to experience wellness we must align with nature's way.

Today's practice is to **LISTEN TO YOUR BODY!**

On a scale from 1-10 answer the following: (1= Not at all & 10 = Yes, completely)

How disempowered do you feel when it comes to your health?
1 2 3 4 5 6 7 8 9 10

How often does your energy and wellness dictate your ability to do things you want to do?

1   2   3   4   5   6   7   8   9   10

How much would your life change if you had better health?

1   2   3   4   5   6   7   8   9   10

*Results: Any score above a 1 on any of your three responses is a *Divine* sign to *Awaken* to the *Truth* of who you are!

➢ What limiting beliefs do you have about health and wellness (Examples: Everyone gets sick. Poor health is just part of getting older)?

➢ What limiting beliefs did your parents tell you about health through the words they spoke and their actions (Examples: Everybody eats junk food and battles with their weight. Exercising is not fun. When you get sick you always take medication)?

➢ What did culture tell you about health and wellness? What did movies tell you about health? What did the media tell you about health? What did your friends tell you about health and wellness (Examples: It's fun to eat junk food. Partying with drugs and alcohol is normal in our culture)?

> ➢ If you had superb energy, what would you spend your time doing?

On a scale from 1-10 answer the following: (1= Not at all & 10 = Yes, completely)

How much do you believe your thoughts and emotions affect your health?
1 2 3 4 5 6 7 8 9 10

How much do you believe you have the choice to eat whole foods and live in alignment with Mother Nature?
1 2 3 4 5 6 7 8 9 10

How much do you believe you deserve to live a life of high energy and vitality?
1 2 3 4 5 6 7 8 9 10

*Results: Add up your scores. Any score below 30 is a *Divine* sign to *Awaken* to the *Truth* of who you are.

What is the impact and probable outcome of your health if you don't do your inner spiritual work to release limiting beliefs, emotions, and align with Mother Nature (Examples: If I don't release my emotions I will keep binging on junk food to fulfill the void within. My vitality will keep getting worse and I won't have the energy to do the things I love to do)?

Day 28

The Cause: The Culmination of Consciousness

There is no illness of the body apart from the mind.

~Socrates

In the spring of 2010, I had a couple of clients I was putting through a sauna detoxification program. One of them had struggled with drugs throughout life and the other just felt the need to cleanse the body to get more energy. As I witnessed the two of them over the course of this intense program in which they took niacin, supplements, oil, and tons of water, they both began to have very interesting side effects. The one client who had taken drugs began to experience the feeling of being high while in the sauna. The drugs that he had consumed over his lifetime began to dislodge from his fat, entered his system, and flushed out through the skin and organs. The other client who was primarily cleansing for high energy said that he began to experience feeling better than he ever had in his entire adult life. Another thing happened: his thinning hair began to have spontaneous re-growth. When the two of their cleansing and detox programs were complete, they both proclaimed that their senses were magnified; their sight was better, their taste buds were amplified, and their energy was dramatically raised. Now, when I'm working with clients, I begin with a cleanse because it impacts their entire *Awakening* process. The point is, when we cleanse the body of the burden of toxins, we free the energy within so it can work its magic with more ease. The body has an intelligence, an automated *Consciousness* designed for well-being.

We all want good health and to look and feel great. This can only be accomplished through one thing: through your *Awakening*. The body is born with wisdom capable of restoring harmony, well-being, and vibrant vitality. When the body is bogged down with toxins and negative emotions, it cannot function properly. When you cleanse the body of negative emotions, negative relationships and chaotic lifestyles, remove yourself from a toxic environment, and avoid poisonous foods, it is then freed to *Awaken*, restoring health and wellness.

The extent to which we individually, culturally, and collectively learn to live in alignment with the natural laws of the *Universe,* will be the extent to which we will experience wellness. You are an eternal immortal spiritual being. You are a soul living in a physical body.

Ridding the body, mind, and lifestyle of impurities is the first step to vibrant health. Just as you cannot be afraid and love in the same thought, you cannot have optimum health in the same body that is burdened with toxins.

Dr. Alexander Haskell N.D. has a simple analogy of a scale. At birth, the scale is tipped to the right, which represents health.

On the right side is all that is beneficial to our physical and mental health, such as nutrient-rich foods, sunshine, positive emotions, and relaxation. On the left side is all that is harmful, such as pollutants, toxins, and stress, and when these begin to outweigh those on the right, the scale tips towards the left, and we begin to experience physical and mental symptoms. Body, mind, and *Spirit* cleansing is an absolute must to experience wellness (A. Haskell, Personal Communication, June 8, 2016).

The second step is to live an authentic life, to align your thinking, actions, and dreams in accordance to your heart's desires. The necessary action for all energy to flow within the body is to unify the *Conscious Mind* with the *Subconscious Mind*. The *Conscious Mind* includes aspects of the body such as the cerebrospinal system, while the *Subconscious Mind* includes the body's autonomic nervous system (ANS); sympathetic, para-sympathetic, and limbic systems. The *Conscious Mind* and *Subconscious Mind* communicate in the core of the body where the vagus nerve meets the ganglionic mass at the rear of the stomach, known as the solar plexus ("Solar Plexus," 2001). When you do not live in alignment, your *Truth* energy is suppressed and must implode within, causing disease. This includes any resistance in your thinking, feelings, or emotions. Any interruption of the free flow of energy will be experienced as unpleasant sensations. Intuitively, you know when you are not in alignment with your highest calling through this center point within your body. You either express or repress energy, setting into motion the creation of vitality or illness.

Google, a universally accessible information company with resonating global success, has employed over 120 internal trainers delivering *The Energy Project*. It entails a way of working to achieve optimum results with a primary mission of helping assist people in having the highest energy and the most productivity by renewing the four core energy needs: physical, emotional, mental, and spiritual. *Spirit* communicates through the body if you are in alignment with the natural laws or not by the experience of your energy levels and health ("The Energy," 2016).

But it is not just obesity, anxiety, and depression that can impact and impede your health so dramatically. Even more startlingly, the findings from the President's Three Person Cancer Panel reported to the U.S. President that approximately 41 % of Americans will be diagnosed with cancer during their lifetime, and around 21 % will die from cancer; however, research on environmental causes of cancer has been limited as it is low in priority and inadequately funded ("President's Cancer," n.d.). We are still not truly focused on the cause of cancer and how our environment and experience triggers and encourages its growth.

Western medicine has created an impressive array of technology in the realm of diagnostics. They are masters of treating symptoms, but have gotten off track with their endeavors of getting to the root causes of illness. I believe when Western Medicine, Preventative and Alternative Medicine, and Spirituality come together, we will have the best healthcare system in history, and maybe even immortality in a physical life form. Having said that, I also believe we are experiencing the breakdown before the breakthrough. People point their fingers at the greed of the pharmaceutical companies, the politics of the hospital and insurance systems, and deaths due to medical complications. Ultimately, we are all in this together via our *Collective Consciousness* and the choices we make.

All Dis-ease is Spiritual

Most of our culture has chosen to be brainwashed by the materialist stating that our health is predisposed by our genes. According to Bruce Lipton in *The Biology of Belief*, genes are only responsible for approximately five to ten percent of the destiny of our health. He states we are not victims of our genes. Lipton also indicates that the chemistry of the body controls the fate and genetics of the cell, and that chemistry is related to the mind's interpretation of the world, which fosters chemistry (Lipton, 2015). Your beliefs create your interpretation of life.

The extent to which you live in accordance with Mother Nature and *Universal Law* as individuals and as a culture, equals the extent to which you will experience health. If you create a world lacking love, community, and intimacy, you go against your spiritual nature. You need each other and neglecting your basic human needs ends in apathy, sadness, loneliness, and poor chemistry. Moreover, we are living under stressful lifestyles. Negative emotions are deadly to the body. They create cortisol which pumps adrenaline in a fight or flight manner.

According to Dr. Andrew Weil, M.D. (2016), nearly one-half of all adults suffer adverse effects from stress. Stress has been linked to all the leading causes of death such as cardiovascular disease, cancer, accidents, and suicide. Almost 90% of all visits to primary healthcare providers are due to stress related problems. When you become acutely stressed you go into a "fight or flight response," releasing such chemicals as adrenaline and norepinephrine which causes inflammation and inhibits the body's ability to heal ("Psychologist," n.d.). Your *Consciousness* creates your belief systems, your belief systems create your feelings, and your feelings create your emotions of pleasure or stress.

Every illness is caused from *Consciousness*; individually, collectively, and universally. Individually, we choose to live stressful lives through our belief systems, our sedentary lifestyle, the things we choose to put into our bodies, and the lifestyles we live. When we take a pill instead of doing our internal *Conscious* work, we suffer the consequences. The *Collective Consciousness* has also created a world of toxicity; EMF's, GMO's, pesticides, chlorine in our water, fluoride in our toothpaste, and pollution in our air. It is ultimately up to you to make a choice.

Day 28 Practice

ALIGN WITH MOTHER NATURE

LAW OF MENTALISM

There is a Divine source and intelligence inherent in all of life. It establishes and regulates the phenomenon of how elemental forms of matter relate. This law dictates the chemistry, biology, and science of the mechanics of this world. This natural design brings structure and standardization to create in a context of organization.

Today's practice is to **ALIGN WITH MOTHER NATURE!**

Pick one of the following:

➢ Go for a walk in a park.

➢ Watch the sunrise or sunset.

➢ Make a meal with whole food from Mother Nature.

➢ Swim in a lake or the ocean.

Day 29

Healing: The Innate Wisdom Within

Simplicity is the ultimate sophistication.

~Leonardo da Vinci

Just as *Consciousness* can cause disease, it can also create good health and well-being. The same energy that can back us up against the wall of an incurable disease is the same energy that creates an Olympic champion. The ideal scenario is to create a culture that nurtures and teaches our children how to consciously live from day one, but unfortunately this is not the case of the modern world. The question is, "how do we go beyond the toxic world to set ourselves free?" First, we must believe that anything is possible.

In 1993, the Institute of Noetic Sciences published *Spontaneous Remission*; an Annotated Bibliography. In this work, the authors, Caryle Hirshberg and the late Brendan O'Regan, defined spontaneous remission as "the disappearance, complete or incomplete, of a disease or cancer without medical treatment or treatment that is considered inadequate to produce the resulting disappearance of disease symptoms or tumor." This project included the largest database of medically reported cases of spontaneous remission in the world, with more than 3,500 references from more than 800 journals in 20 different languages. So, how did these Spontaneous Remissions occur? Trained at Harvard, Dr. Kelly Turner, Ph.D., set out to find the answer by traveling the world and interviewing the patients and alternative healers of these cases and found that it was not luck, but rather intensely proactive actions that influenced the outcomes. In radical remission, Dr. Kelly concluded there were nine healing factors:

(a) radically change your diet, (b) take control of your health, (c) follow your intuition, (d) use herbs and supplements, (e) release suppressed emotions, (f) increase positive emotions, (g) embrace social support, (h) deepen your spiritual connection, and (i) have strong reasons for living.

Given that it is impossible to heal under stressful lifestyles, what would it look like to live in alignment with Mother Nature and the *Universal Laws*? Hippocrates said that nature itself is the best physician ("Hippocrates," n.d.). When you align the body, mind, and *Spirit* with the natural *Laws of the Universe* and express your unique *Divine Truth*, you experience ultimate vibrancy. You embody magnetism, charisma, and longevity. When the solar plexus is unified, the universal energy is at the individual's beck and call. There appears to be unlimited resources for healing and revitalization. It is the highest *Consciousness* that causes *Spontaneous Recovery* and ultimately, a life of wellness. To reach your highest *Consciousness*, you must focus and make a dedicated effort to expand.

Day 29 Practice

RELAX AND REJUVENATE

LAW OF HEALING

Healing is done through the revealing of Truth. You have the power to heal through the power of your mind. You have been endowed with an infinite intelligence and an innate healer within. Aligning with Mother Nature and the Universal Laws allows the symptoms to go away. Negativity, toxicity, and stress, are all the indicators you are not aligned.

Today's practice is to **RELAX AND REJUVINATE!**

Journal for 10 minutes:

➢ Ask yourself, how could I lower the stress in my life (Example: Maybe you could leave ten minutes early for work so you don't get stressed due to traffic)?

➢ When could you say "no" to simplify your day (Example: Say no to social media and turn on some classical music and relax)?

➢ What could you do today to relax and rejuvenate (Example: Take a bubble bath)?

Purpose & Calling

Day 30

The Call: Transforming Suffering to Victory

The meaning of life is to find your gift. The purpose of life is to give it away.

~Pablo Picasso

There are moments in life when something happens; life alters, and your entire perception transforms instantaneously. For me, that moment was 22 years ago when I was holding my stillborn son in my arms, just after giving birth to him. Tears were streaming down my face as I looked at his beautiful body and realized his body was still there, but he wasn't. I understood he wasn't his body; he is a spiritual being. One can conceptually grasp the concept that we are not these bodies, but I captured it on an entirely different level. My world crumbled, delivering me to spiritual revelation. This experience sent me on an intense spiritual quest that led to my life's calling.

I never in a million years thought I would become a Doctor of *Divinity* and teach spirituality. My only intention was to heal myself from the suffering I was experiencing within and to discover my true essence; but year after year of living my daily spiritual practice, learning the greatest philosophies, and embodying the revelations, my calling was birthed.

The blessing of adversity resides in the transformation of suffering into victory. This is the shift within your *Consciousness* to understand how life is always unfolding for you to *Awaken* to your *purpose* and *calling*.

Many people come to me trying to figure out their purpose and calling. They are constantly seeking it out in the world, thinking that if they just attend more conferences, get another coach, or take another class, then they will figure out their calling. In my personal experience assisting others in the birthing of their calling, I find that it is always given from within. It's whispered from the depths of the soul in silence.

Not everyone must go through something traumatic to discover their purpose and calling; however, many people are seeking to find their unique gift to give to the world. They realize it is not as easy as ordering off a menu. You must clear out the social dogma and let go of what your parents told you that you should do. You must release all mind chatter, paying close attention to the sounds of *the calling* from the depths of your soul. Out of the morass emerges a knowing within, like a whisper from the chambers of the heart. Once it is heard, you can no longer deny your destiny, but you can still stay detached from the outcome. When you know your calling, you simply live your *Truth*. You become the very essence of your purpose. It is your conversation, your focus, your joy. It is who you are.

In our culture, we have placed such significance on our careers. People have a relentless infatuation with "what we do," which stifles the beautiful process of expression. We find ourselves like deer in headlights, stuck in the paradox of choice, putting pressure on ourselves to figure it out. Finding your purpose and calling is a profoundly liberating experience. It is easier than you make it out to be. Once again, you must *Empty the Consciousness* of the box you have put yourself in, letting go of the concept of who you are in the realm of gifts, talents, and capabilities. Often, you get the call from life through some bizarre incidence. Many times, the most difficult experience you endure becomes the exact situation that leads to your purpose and calling. This is the transformative spiritual gift.

This is the paradox of life and suffering. In some strange twist, it is working for your evolution towards love and connection. Inspirational people like Anne Frank, Joan of Arc, Terry Waite, and Nelson Mandela, are just a few who have endured the darkest depths of human suffering, and yet carved a beauty in their wake more powerful than any of their suppressors. I can certainly testify that the darkest moments of our lives can be the biggest blessing if we use them as impetus to send us on the greatest spiritual journey. It has become my purpose and calling to assist you in your *Awakening*, transform your suffering, and birth your *purpose and calling*. You cannot avoid suffering, but you can choose how to find meaning in it and how to cope with it as you move forward.

Day 30 Practice

LIVE WITH PURPOSE

LAW OF DHARMA

This law states that each person has a special gift, a unique purpose and message to bring to the world. You have a unique talent that no other individual in the world has. Through the intention of working for the highest good and out of service, this law unlocks the Divine within. The entire cosmos has aligned for you to take on a physical form to fulfill this calling. There's a message and a gift within you that the world thirsts for. You are the only person in the entire Universe with this Divine purpose. Your Divine purpose is your destiny.

Today's practice is to **LIVE WITH PURPOSE!**

Talents + Passions + Triumphs = Purpose

➢ Make a list of your skills, talents, and knowledge.

➢ Make a list of your passions and potential ways you could turn your passions into valuable services.

➢ Make a list of the hardest experiences you've ever gone through and list the victories you've had over these challenges.

➢ Make a list of how you feel you could help others who are going through a similar situation.

Day 31

The Opus: Leaving Your Legacy

Everyone has a purpose in life... a unique gift or special talent to give to others. And when we blend this unique talent with service to others, we experience the ecstasy and exultation of our own spirit, which is the ultimate goal of all goals.

~Deepak Chopra

Antonio Lucio Vivaldi was born on March 4, 1678 in Venice, Italy. He was considered one of the most renowned classical composers to have lived. The prolific artist left this life with hundreds of pieces of grand symphonies, concertos, and masterpieces. His story begins as a little boy who loved the violin, playing with his father and famous musicians. He became an ordained priest, but didn't last long due to his love of his art.

Vivaldi was a master teacher of *The Law of Eternality*. He left a legacy; a body of work and gifts to this life that live beyond his lifetime. This law states that your true essence has no beginning or end because who you are a ceaseless creative source. There is no space or time in the spiritual realm; there is only one life, one mind, one *Spirit*. Healing and heaven are in the present moment. This immutable and unchangeable aspect of you is the part of you that is eternal. You are immortal.

Vivaldi embodied his work at such a profound level that he became an icon of classical music. He lived it, breathed it, loved it, created it, and gave his gift away to the world everywhere he went. In doing so, he was recognized, and loved for his gift of music. What people might not know about Vivaldi is that his talent did not necessarily translate into financial success, but a life full of riches.

The Opus is the legacy you leave behind in this lifetime. Douglas Vermeeren produced the movie The Opus. He said The Opus is about creating your own personal legacy. What will you do during your brief time on Earth? What will you be remembered for? Will this planet be a better place because you were here? How can you accomplish the things you dream about most and create that grand legacy? Every person born on the planet arrives with the potential to create an incredible legacy. But only some people do.

What do you want to be remembered for? What do you want to spend your time in this lifetime doing? What do you want to embody? What do you desire to experience? Who do you have to become to live that vision? The *Law of Attraction* is not about sitting in meditation envisioning what you desire; it is the embodiment of that which you desire to experience. If you desire to be wealthy, then be someone who embodies great wisdom of how to create wealth and make others wealthy. If you desire to be an Oscar winning actor, then embody the skills to be the best possible actor. If you desire to experience love, then be the most loving person you know. You are not here to win a race of materialism. You are here to experience the depths of your soul in form. Potentially the highest yield is to measure yourself by the number of people that you touch in this life, or maybe it is to produce the experience of being fully alive. No matter the vision, what you embody is what form your life takes on. You are the greatest production. Be legendary!

The Silent Revolution

There is a *Silent Revolution* happening within the hearts and souls of people across the world. People are *Awakening*; values are shifting and morals are realigning. There is an actual movement happening across the globe of a genre of people called the *Cultural Creative*. This includes people who are either conscious in the running of their business or desiring to make a difference through their careers and companies. There are around 50 million people considered to be a part of this movement in the United States alone and millions more around the world. But this is not your typical revolution; it is one of the heart that starts from deep within; it is a calling, a silent whisper from *Spirit* for a better way. People are tired of the game of deceit and manipulation, of trying to keep up with 'The Joneses'. The system is broken. We no longer want to win at a game where you never get what you truly desire, which is love and connection. My personal journey has been one of *Awakening* to true wealth: the abundant source that is within. I have experienced having an abundance of monetary wealth, yet felt bankrupt inside, realizing that until one understands that true wealth comes from *Source*, one will forever be chasing a fleeting illusion. My entrepreneurial skills combined with my unshakable spirituality, have brought me to a life beyond my wildest dreams. Let us consider the principles of *Conscious Commerce*; networking and building relationships that not only serve you, but also serve the highest good, all while adhering to your *Divine* birthright of abundance, prosperity, and liberation. Giving the world the gift of the greatest version of you coupled with providing service to others, is the ultimate *Purpose and Calling*.

The topic of *Purpose and Calling* often gets entangled with the fascinating topic of money. To recap, money is a fantastic symbol and projection of your current state of mind and *Consciousness*; it can represent fun, security, power, triumph, abundance, or even failure. Every person has an individualistic set of beliefs and meanings when it comes to the concept of money and wealth. Some people feel angst, anxiety, disempowerment, and inadequacy when it comes to money. Others feel freedom, empowerment, creativity, and excitement. There are the greedy, the manipulative, and the fearful in the realm of monetary wealth. We find ourselves like rats on a wheel going around and around, only to realize we aren't getting anywhere, just deeper in debt. Our culture is obsessed by material worth and gain. What is the measurement of status? As a stigma, men define themselves by what they do and how much money they make. It is vital that you shift your values and learn to prosper through extraordinary relationships in your life. Release thoughts of scarcity and feelings of fear by powerfully stepping into a prosperous mentality and lifestyle.

True wealth is your very essence; you are an abundant spiritual being, infinite innovator, and an extraordinary creator.

You are worth more than all the money on this planet and you have the potential to expand your *Consciousness* and have more wisdom than all the libraries in the world combined. Wealth is a state of being, which means you bring wealth to everything and everyone. Wealth is being helpful everywhere you go; it is serving, giving and expressing, and in that way of being, the world reflects to you that which you are.

Day 31 Practice

LIVE WITH INTENTION

LAW OF ETERNALITY

Your true essence has no beginning or end because who you are is the ceaseless creative source. There is no space or time in the spiritual realm; there is only one life, one mind, one Spirit. Healing and heaven are in the present moment. This immutable and unchangeable aspect of you is the part of you that is eternal. You are immortal.

Today's practice is to **LIVE WITH INTENTION!**

➢ What limiting beliefs do you have about creative expression and dreaming (Examples: Only delusional people dream. Only artists are creative. I'm too old to fulfill my dreams)?

➢ What limiting beliefs did your parents instill in you about creative expression and dreaming through the words they spoke and their actions (Examples: My parents both worked in jobs they hated. My father said that he had to grow up and pay the bills)?

➢ What did your culture tell you about being creative? What did the movies tell you about dreaming? What did the media tell you about creative expression? What did your friends tell you about being creative (Examples: I learned though my culture that very few people realize their dreams. Many of my friends gave up on their dreams when they had children. One of my friends accomplished his dream of becoming an artist, but also became an alcoholic)?

➢ List the times you handed your power over to "doing the right thing" instead of taking the risk and going after your dreams (Example: I remember the time I settled for a decent paying job instead of fulfilling my dreams).

➢ If you had all the time in the world, what would you spend your time doing?

➢ Where in life do you lose track of time because you love what you are doing so much?

➢ What unique gifts can you bring to the world?

Take ten minutes to journal:

➢ What would you like to be remembered for?

➢ Will the world be a better place because of you?

➢ Whose lives would you like to positively impact?

➢ What would you like to master in this lifetime?

Step IV:

AFFIRM

Day 32

Creating Your Life's Purpose Statement

Until one is committed, there is hesitancy, the chance to draw back, always ineffectiveness. Concerning all acts of initiative (and creation), there is one elementary truth, the ignorance of which kills countless ideas and splendid plans: that the moment one definitely commits oneself, then Providence moves too. All sorts of things occur to help one that would never otherwise have occurred. A whole stream of events issues from the decision, raising in one's favor all manner of unforeseen incidents and meetings and material assistance, which no man could have dreamt would have come his way. Whatever you can do or dream you can, begin it. Boldness has genius, power and magic in it.

~Goethe

One day I asked an artist friend of mine, "When did you start to love art?" He began to tell me a story of when he was a little boy and went over to a neighbor's house, a man he referred to as one of the nicest people he had ever met. The gentleman toured him around his house, taking him into his garage which had been converted into an art studio. There were big pieces of wood; some were on the ground and some were hanging. He came to this magnificent wood carving in the middle of the room. The man, a wood sculptor, proceeded to tell him how he would chip away everything that was not in the form that he envisioned.

My friend, who is a *Song of the Year Grammy Winner*, went on to say that he was profoundly moved by the concept of envisioning a piece of art in your head and then chipping away everything that is not part of that vision. He said that this was one of the greatest lessons he ever learned: *The Art of Simplifying.*

Discovering your *Life's Purpose Statement* is a process of becoming *The Sculptor of Your Life*. You simplify, you disentangle from the things you do not want, you chip away the chaos, you deconstruct suffering, and you follow your bliss. You clean up, you clear up, you cut down, and you release the frills and unravel from that which no longer serves you. You become the mathematician that deciphers computations to see the base of the equation. You become the scientist that boils down the substance to the primary factors. You become the therapist that peels back the layers of the onion to the heart of the matter. Simplicity is an art. Simplicity is a path to *Awakening*.

To gain clarity on your *Life's Purpose Statement*, you must first understand your own personal *Truth*. Throughout my journeys, all my travels, teachings, a plethora of books, and first-hand witnessing of real live human beings, I began to observe those who seemed to be the most fulfilled and happy in their existence. There was a common denominator of the people who had *Awakened* to their *Life's Purpose*. These where the people who were directly living their principles; not categorical principles or set dogma, in fact, many had no dogma at all, but those people were simply living in alignment with their own personal *Truth*. These are the people who seem to live without angst or turmoil within; those who have closed the gap between who they want to be and who they are. Their actions match their principles. What does it take for people to close the gap between themselves as they are and who they want to be? I started to look at different spiritual exercises of our indigenous ancestors, realizing that their rituals, ceremonies, and practices help to keep them in alignment with their commitments and *Life's Purpose*.

Knowing that you are a habitual being, you can re-train your mind to focus on what you want instead of focusing on what you do not want. Next, you re-train your voice and your choice of words to powerfully create your world into existence. Finally, you re-train the way you live to consistently be in alignment with what you desire to experience. You can create exercises for yourself to incorporate habits that are in direct alignment with all that you truly desire. There are several tools you can use to do this.

The goal is to create your *Life's Purpose Statement* to achieve clarity and understanding of your life. Learning to simplify your life will allow the space for the internal wisdom to emerge. Asking yourself heartfelt questions regarding what truly matters to you will allow your Higher-Self to assist you in developing your *Life's Purpose Statement*.

Throughout history, sculptors describe chipping away everything that is not a part of their vision. By getting rid of what they did not want, they created exactly what they originally envisioned. Most of you do not wake up one day with a perfectly laid out vision for your life. Sometimes you know exactly what you want, and other times, it takes work to uncover what it is you truly need.

Consider that creating your *Life's Purpose Statement* can be a counterintuitive process; the opposite of *figuring it out*. It is like being a wood sculptor, chipping away and clearing out everything that is not within your bliss. When you do not know what to envision for your life, become the sculptor, revealing your perfect path. Create your ultimate masterpiece. Ancient Zen saying states, "close your eyes to see clearly, be still and you will hear the *Truth*."

In the next section, I will guide you through a series of exercises that will help you *Awaken* to your *Life's Purpose Statement*.

Step One: Simplify

Distractions are the kryptonite of clarity. When you simplify, you begin to decrease confusion, allowing something to emerge from the silence. When you simplify, your life drowns out the noise of the world and begins to discern what does and does not work for you. In the clearing of the chaos, you are left with clarity. Removing yourself from all the moving parts of your daily routine gives you an opportunity to simplify. Vacations can help in attaining clarity.

Step Two: Clarity

Gain clarity on your *'must haves'* in your life. You can ask yourself, "Where in life do I lose track of time?", "When I am looking back on my life from my death-bed, what would I regret if I had not done it?", "What are the things in life that I value the most?" Through this process of reflection and introspection, you become clear on what YOU value. You do not have to wait for a tragic accident or life-threatening situation to shift your values and force you to assess your priorities; you can consciously address them every single day.

Step Three: Envision

When most people think of a *Life's Purpose Statement* or *Vision*, they think of creating goals or some ideal scene. Envisioning is not another projection from your ego or a vision board of material belongings you desire; it is a process of allowing your Higher-Self to deliver your vision to you. You can do this by asking more questions within meditation periods or during times when you make it a point to silence your mind. When in silence, ask your Higher-Self, "What is my *Unique Divine Expression* and gift to the world? What is the vision for how I will give the world the gifts that I possess? How can I be a benefit to all individuals that I encounter? What knowledge and what gifts can I use to positively impact the world?" This is the *Law of Dharma* in expression.

Step Four: Specificity

Be specific with your *Life's Purpose Statement* and *Vision*. Write down exactly what your vision is in detail. Play it so vividly within your mind that you can describe it as if it is already real. Clarity is power. When you are waking in the morning and when you are dozing off to sleep at night, spend time visioning.

Imagine all the sensations of the manifestation and demonstration of your life in full bloom. Make a vision board or keep pictures in your phone that represent it so you can look at it multiple times a day.

Step Five: Focus

Stayed focused and stay in integrity. This is a process of saying *no* to anything that is no longer in alignment with the clarity and focus of your *Life's Purpose Statement* and *Vision*. This is the process of' following your bliss and allowing your life to unfold through the clarity of the present moment. Every day, use the *Law of Intention* and desire to demonstrate and manifest your visions into form. Life becomes easy and flows as you allow your natural love to direct each decision.

Day 32 Practice

CREATE YOUR LIFE'S PURPOSE STATEMENT

LAW OF DESIRE OR DESTINY

What you truly desire is your destiny. Your greatest will is that which prevails within your life. It is the sum of your Consciousness and actions. At the core of you is the creator of your destiny of the physical realm, a unique Divine design. The extent to which you have clarity of your desires and specifically inform Universal Law, is the extent to which you will experience the destiny you consciously desire.

Today's practice is to **CREATE YOUR LIFE'S PURPOSE STATEMENT!**

You came to this world to bring your specific gifts and talents. The first step in discovering your purpose and calling is to BECOME THE SCULPTOR OF YOUR LIFE by simplifying and saying no to everything that doesn't speak to your heart.

Say "Yes" to all the things you love.

Say "No" to all the things you don't love.

Make a list of all the things you spend time doing and put them into two categories:

> ➤ Love
> ➤ Don't love

Schedule the things you love to do right now.

Create Your *Life's Purpose* Statement:

Creating a *Life's Purpose Statement* is a commitment to oneself. It is something that you read at the beginning of each day to stay powerfully focused on what you are committed to in your life. It is your North Star, guiding you every step of the way. It helps you to stay in alignment with your intentions, stay in your own integrity every day, and stand in your unique *Truth*. It is a fantastic way of getting into the mindset for the day so that you can embody that which you desire to be.

Your *Life's Purpose Statement* Must Include the Following:

> ➤ Write your purpose statement in present tense, as if it has already been manifested and demonstrated.
> ➤ Write your purpose statement in measurable and obtainable affirmations.
> ➤ Write your purpose statement in four sentences that address the four areas of your life.
> ➤ Write your purpose statement in a positive manner.
> ➤ Write what you will give in exchange for your financial abundance and the life you desire.

Examples of Life Purpose Statements:

Example 1:

Health & Wellness: I have radiant health, eat whole foods, and love fitting into my clothes with comfort.

Relationships & Love: I celebrate my thriving family and peaceful friends.

Money & Career: I live the life of my dreams with $250k a year from my writing career.

Creative Expression: I am honored to deliver beautiful books to the world every year.

What I give in exchange for my financial abundance: I provide phenomenal writing and editing services.

Example 2:

Health & Wellness: I love daily exercise, energizing, and revitalizing my body.

Relationships & Love: I love my extraordinary partner and spiritual community of friends.

Money & Career: I live abundantly on 10k a month from my investments in real estate.

Creative Expression: I joyously give my art to the world without attachment.

What I give in exchange for my financial abundance: I deliver clean housing for people to live in.

Example 3:

Health & Wellness: I love my balanced life of wellness, living vegan, and toxin free.

Relationships & Love: I am so grateful for my divine partner and my technological community.

Money & Career: I live in full prosperity on $100k a year doing what I love to do in film.

Creative Expression: Every day I get to create epic films that positively impact the world.

What I give in exchange for my financial abundance: I awaken the world through enlightening movies.

Your Life's Purpose Statement:

On or before (date): _____

Health & Vitality:

_____

_____

_____

_____

Money & Career:

_____

_____

_____

_____

Love & Relationships:

_____

_____

_____

_____

Creative Expression:

_____

_____

_____

_____

(Write your *Life's Purpose Statement* on the back of a 3x5 index card and carry it everywhere you go, reading it at least three times a day).

State what you will give in exchange for your financial abundance.

Example:

What I will give in exchange for the life that I desire is to *Awaken* people to their *Divinity*, their *Life's Purpose*, and assist them in manifesting their dreams by providing inspirational and empowering programs.

Example: (This is Andrew Carnegies' Exchange statement)
"Assembling and publicizing the principles by which great individuals achieve enduring success."

What Will You Give in Exchange for Your Financial Abundance?

_____

_____

_____

_____

_____

Day 33

Creating Your Daily Spiritual Practice

The world will persist in exhibiting before you what you persist in affirming the world is.

~ Emma Curtis Hopkins

A mentor of mine once told me a poignant story relating to the value of practice. I'm not sure if it was true or not, but regardless, it made the point. He said that there was a lady in New York who was on her way to Carnegie Hall for a concert. She was running late and realized she wasn't sure how to get there. She began to get a little frazzled, walking faster and faster, as she kept turning corners in the city, only to fail to see the famous concert hall. Suddenly, she saw a man about to get into a cab who happened to be the singer Luciano Pavarotti, but the woman didn't recognize who he was. She abruptly asked with immense anxiety, "Excuse me sir, do you know how to get to Carnegie Hall?" He replied with great peace and a jovial poise, "practice, practice, practice."

I giggled when my wise friend made his point through the punch line of that story: practice, practice, practice. I could only imagine how much practice Pavarotti had to do to be such a master of his craft; one of the most famous Italian opera singers ever. The story makes the case that even the greatest artists must practice.

Having a Daily Spiritual Practice is the path to your *Awakening*. There are as many different types of practices as there are people. It is important for you to design one that is right for you. Throughout the next seven chapters we go over the primary types of spiritual practices: Meditation, Mindfulness, Language, Visioning, Intuition, Affirmative Prayer and Affirmations, and 40-Day Practices.

You may choose to have a morning and evening ritual, or you may prefer to only practice once a day. You may create rituals with people you love or do your practice alone. You may join a yoga class and do your affirmations and meditation within the confines of a community. You may simply choose to be mindful of your thoughts and how you speak your world into existence. Your practices could be simple or regimented. You create your own spiritual practice, at your pace, and at your will. Just make sure that it is genuine and comes from your heart. Daily spiritual practices are a way of life.

Daily Spiritual Practice – A Way of Life!

Wealth & Wisdom:

Goal: Powerful & Productive
Action: Allow the abundance of life to flow through you, as you. Focus on innovation and collaboration. Shift your mind to one of service and gratitude. Set time aside to advance your skillset and expertise. Embody the mindset it takes to fulfill upon your

dreams. Take bold action that is driven by your mission and purpose statement. Shift problems into opportunities. Commit to being the best version of yourself. Build assets, create community, and leverage your extraordinary relationships. Reprogram your *Subconscious Mind* by demanding and commanding that which you seek.

Release: The limited belief that money is more powerful than you. Let go of your scarcity mindset and doing business with people who bring you down.

Love & Relationships:

Goal: Peace & Connection

Action: Focus on developing the relationship with your Higher-Self. Seek to remove all the barriers within yourself that stand between you and love. Choose to focus on people's strengths and attributions. Allow people to show up in their divinity; having authentic and positive conversations that allow for transformation. Seek to understand others viewpoints before trying to be understood. Learn to create boundaries with people who aren't in alignment with harmony and love. Surround yourself with positive people who are committed to growth.

Release: Let go of the need to make others wrong. Stop participating in activities that bring you suffering; fixing or changing others; engaging in dysfunctional or chaotic situations; doing the same thing over and over expecting a different outcome.

Health & Wellness:

Goal: High Energy & Radiance

Action: Focus on raising the vibration of your body through spiritual connection, whole foods, and physical exercise. Take time to cleanse and detoxify the body. Set time aside for relaxation and rejuvenation. Engage with Mother Nature; take hikes, swim in the ocean, or walk in the park; revitalize your body with good rest, pure water, and nutritious supplements.

Release: Eating processed and junk foods; toxifying and clogging the natural ability of the body; let go of your causes of stress and circumstances that raise your blood pressure and restrict the flow of blood throughout your system.

Purpose & Calling:

Goal: Self-Expression & Creativity

Action: Go within, quiet your mind, and seek your truth. Transform suffering into victory; taking a look at the most challenging things you've gone through and celebrating the lessons you've learned. Focus on your talents, passions, and triumphs. Give yourself fully to life by giving your gifts and message to the world. Leave your legacy by giving your art, service, and love. Embody that which you seek.

Release: Let go of the desire for validation or the need to be acknowledged by people. Stop focusing on the lack of production and start asking yourself who you are being.

The Promise

❖ I Promise to be still and know the *Truth*.

❖ I Promise to only speak the *Truth* of abundant health, happiness, prosperity, and love.

❖ I Promise to be one with all, so that nothing can disturb my peace of mind.

❖ I Promise to stand for the *Truth* that everyone is *Divine*.

❖ I Promise to focus on the positive and optimistic side of life and circumstances.

❖ I Promise to think only of *Divine*, to work only for *Divine*, and to expect *Divinity*.

❖ I Promise to give a gift wherever I go and to whomever I encounter.

❖ I Promise to dedicate an abundant amount of energy to the expanding of my *Consciousness*.

❖ I Promise to declare the *Truth* and release all worry, anger, hurt, and fear.

❖ I Promise to focus on happiness, to release my troubles, and to stop complaining.

❖ I Promise to have faith that the *Universe* is working at all points in time for the highest good.

❖ I Promise to allow these *Truth*s through my daily spiritual practice and connection to *Source*.

❖ I Promise to vibrantly live the *Truth* today and every day.

Day 33 Practice

CREATE YOUR DAILY SPIRITUAL PRACTICE

LAW OF ACTION

Newton's Third Law states, "For every action, there is an equal and opposite reaction." The Universe is a non-dualistic mechanical system, a unified energetic field. This is how your actions are actively corresponded and reflected to you. With every action you take, you set into motion a cooperative system of infinite magnitude. Every non-action is an action in the realm of Consciousness. For every harmonic and loving action, there is a reciprocation of harmony in one's life. For every chaotic and harmful action, there is payback of chaos in one's life.

Today's practice is to **CREATE YOUR DAILY SPIRITUAL PRACTICE!**

➢ Choose the time(s) of day you are going to engage in your *Daily Spiritual Practice.*

➢ Create a sacred space that is quiet and where you will not be distracted.

➢ Decide what your morning and evening practices will consist of: meditation, journaling, breathwork, yoga, contemplation, visioning, affirmative prayer, affirmations, etc.

➢ Consciously choose how you are going to practice mindfulness throughout the day.

➢ Keep a daily journal on intuition and gratitude (see day 38).

➢ Find a community or spiritual mastermind for support.

Day 34

Meditation: The Infinite Journey

In daily meditation lies the secret power.

~H. Emelie Cady

On May 25, 1955, a new Viharn building at a temple had been constructed to house a 9.8-foot-tall plaster Buddha statue. Rumor has it that during the move, the ropes broke and the statue crashed onto the ground, breaking the outer shell. Underneath, a shining object appeared which turned out to be a pure gold Buddha worth approximately 250 million dollars. The origin of the statue is uncertain, but believed to have been made some time around the 13th or 14th century and then plastered over to prevent its theft from Burmese invaders during the destruction of Ayutthaya Kingdom in 1867.

This Golden Buddha has become a symbol for the *Awakening* that is revealed through meditation. It is said that within all of us is pure gold; an aspect of us that is a precious Buddha. Through the practice of meditation, we chip off a little more of our outer shell that divides us from our purity, and our divine state of Oneness.

Establishing a meditation practice into your daily life can have an immense impact on your *Individual Consciousness* and

Sub-Consciousness, linking you to the *Cosmic Consciousness* through the union of the body, mind, and *Spirit*. This modality can radically alter your perception, understanding, and effect of your circumstances. It can equip you with clarity to make better choices and lead you to increased awareness and centeredness in your decision-making abilities, continually inspiring you to fulfill your unique destiny and birthright. Meditation is a very powerful way to align with *Spirit*.

What is Meditation and How Does It Work?

Meditation is the medium where the individual self and the Higher-Self meet and join into One. It is the uniting of the divided-self with the *Divine*-self. Meditation involves quieting the mind and transcending beyond the ego, into the eternal, the *One Mind*: *Spirit*. There are many types of meditation. These include Transcendental, Contemplative, Reflective, Mantra, Vipassana, Insight, Walking, Tantra, Loving Kindness, Worship, Yoga, Focused Attention, Chakra, Kundalini, Third-eye, Mindful, Gazing, Zen, Breathing, Sound, Singing, and many more. There are hundreds of ways of meditating, and there is no *wrong* way of meditating. People use the sacred space within to do a variety of healings, contemplations, intuitive work, expansion of *Consciousness,* and much more.

Meditation is an infinite adventure of healing, shedding, unveiling, revelation, and *Awakening*. Today, we are faced with an overload of input due to technological advances, often increasing our levels of stress. These levels are further impacted by our everyday lives and our internal and external discord.

Meditation serves you on every possible conceivable level. Its effects are highly regarded and feverously being researched. Meditation is promoted and continually backed by a multitude of solid studies and scientifically based evidence, which indicate that meditation benefits our health, reduces illness, increases productivity, and induces a general positive mental and physical experience (McGreevey, 2012). One study has shown that meditation rebuilds gray matter in eight weeks (Wolfe, 2016). We refer to gray matter as the darker tissue of the brain and spinal cord that mainly consists of nerve cell bodies and branching dendrites, which we most commonly refer to as human intelligence. It is a major component of the central nervous system and directly corresponds to your stress levels, emotional balance, and sensory perception of your environment and experience.

One of the main goals behind meditation is to understand the Spiritual realm better than the Physical realm. When your *Divinity* becomes more real than the circumstances of your life, you are freed from feeling as if you do not have control over your life. You learn the *Truth* that you are in this world, but you are not of this world. According to a study by Harvard Business Review, the two most effective business tools for the twenty-first century executives are meditation and intuition (Seppala, 2015). Today, meditation is becoming not only a standard practice, but also a survival skill for top CEOs across the globe. Meditation is equally relevant for all of us existing in this modern world. Today's culture is tirelessly chaotic; we have much information continuously infiltrating our minds and overloading our senses via the internet, social media, emails, news, media, and the transition of almost every genre of life.

Quieting the mind is an absolute necessity in the modern world. Harvard research, like many brilliant institutions of academic excellence, has found that these skills are integral and essential to the development of the individual, both on a personal level and in the workplace (Seppala, 2015). Corporations are also beginning to recognize the power of mental clarity, minimizing stress, and the aspects of mind over matter.

Stress, anxiety, and feeling overwhelmed, directly impacts our culture. Americans are increasingly obese, disease spreads rampantly, and our inability to maintain balance and a clear view of life sets us back individually and as a race. Illness and depression rise and we become lost in the fog. Meditation has been proven to lower stress, decrease blood pressure, decrease anxiety, improve psychological disorders, and increase mental clarity and concentration.

Researchers at Johns Hopkin's University looked at approximately 19,000 meditation studies. They found 47 studies that met their criteria for solid and well-designed studies. What they found in the analysis of their review is that mindfulness meditation can help ease psychological stressors such as depression, anxiety, and pain (Corliss, 2014). According to Dr. Elizabeth Hoge, a psychiatrist at the Center for Anxiety and Traumatic Stress Disorders at Massachusetts General Hospital, mindfulness meditation is perfect for treating anxiety because people that have anxiety have many distracting thoughts that are very powerful. As a result, people cannot tell the difference between a nagging worrisome thought and a problem-solving thought. She also states that one can train to experience thoughts completely differently. Through mindfulness, one learns to recognize thoughts that are not helpful, leading to an understanding that it is simply a thought and not a part of the core self (Corliss, 2014).

Throughout my career, I have received numerous phone calls from clients seeking ways to manage their overwhelming stress from having to make too many decisions in every aspect of their lives. This is what is known as the Pinball Effect. Typically, these clients are frequently reactive on a day-to-day basis. The ball in a pinball machine represents my clients, bouncing back and forth and up and down each time they are hit with a difficult circumstance. They feel great and on top of the world if everything is going their way, but as soon as anything happens in which appears to impede their success, they react in angst, worry, and anger. Their blood boils over and they rapidly spiral downward into a negative state of isolation, hitting road blocks. Along the way, when something positive happens, their ego gets a boost, and they are back to thinking they have it all figured out. Over time, their anxiety and fear increases, and it is a matter of time before they spiral downward again.

They develop an unnerving feeling of being out of control and they don't know why. Deep inside, they know that their entire world is based on the circumstances of the world out there. Their self-worth is based on their ego identity, what car they are driving, what house they are living in, how much money they have in the bank, and how much admiration they are getting from others. Somewhere deep down inside they know that their foundation of stability is based on the world *out there* and it is unstable. They know that if something major happened, such as a stock market crash, they would go straight into a meltdown. Meditation is crucial in addressing these feelings.

A study by Dr. Ramesh Manocha (2001) at Sydney University found that occupational stress decreased by 26 percent after eight weeks of meditation. There are so many benefits of meditation; quieting the mind, developing new neuron connections between both hemispheres of the brain, lowering stress, ending mind chatter, stabilizing the psyche, learning to observe thoughts instead of being the effect of them, allowing a space for healing and calming, and releasing limited beliefs. Through this modality, you *Empty the Consciousness* and unveil your authentic essence. You are freed from the circumstances of this world and become unshakable, living from the foundation of your Highest *Consciousness*: *Spirit*.

There is no destination within meditation. Some say it can't be taught because it must be experienced. It is a journey. You can only expand as much as you are ready; you can only learn what you are ready to learn; and you can only be guided where you are willing to go. This is the discovery of you and no one can take you there except yourself.

The Observer

One of the greatest gifts you can obtain from meditation is getting in touch with the eternal space within you, shifting values, and experiencing life on an elevated plane. You distinguish the difference between the eternal space within you—the never changing observer to all of life that has always been with you. We refer to it as the *Observer* - it is the presence within you that observes all of life without judgment, never making circumstances *right* or *wrong*. It does not react, it simply observes.

Once you get in touch with the *Observer* through meditation, you can go back out into the world, use this skill, and stay in a state of mind that is non-reactive, nonjudgmental, and not attached to the conditions of life. You can make choices instead of responding with all the strong emotions that can tag along. You are still fully engaged in life, relationships, business, and all aspects of living, yet, you are not the effect of them. You realize your ability to simply choose, creatively create, and express yourself. Of course, life still happens; cars break down, people can be jerks, business goes up and down, but to go through life in turmoil does not do any good. Through meditation you can navigate through life on a more advanced plane with clarity, grace, and dignity. You can be calm amid chaos, and you can make conscious and sound decisions that help you move forward. You stop feeling overwhelmed because you can focus on finding your path, fully connected to your Higher-Self.

Sun Analogy

Meditation plays a key role in expanding your *Consciousness*; broadening your perceptions and experience of life, and allowing the *Universal Truths* to flow to you and through you. You can think about this in terms of sunlight. The sun represents the *Consciousness* of the entire *Universe,* your unbounded *Consciousness,* and your potential to broaden your mind. It is the *Divine* presence, the *Source,* and the *Force* that you are. The sun shines down from the sky, all giving, bringing harmony and order, shining life and energy, feeding the plants and animals, and giving life to all.

Imagine you can see the sun, feel the sun, and you know you are thriving and surviving because of the sun. Now, imagine that there are clouds between you and the sun. The clouds represent all the limited beliefs, all the concepts, identities, perceptions, viewpoints, and your five senses that are condensing and constricting your use of your *Consciousness* [the sun]. As you expand your *Consciousness* and move beyond clouds through meditation, you allow the sun to shine in, bringing the entire wisdom of the *Universe* into your *Consciousness*. You experience being one with the world, feeling moments of enlightenment. You become one with your Higher-Self and can shine back into the world. The ultimate mentor and guru is inside of you. As you bask in the oneness, the wisdom of the cosmos streams in, informing the *Universal Truths.* When this occurs, you experience life on a level beyond anything you have ever known; beyond the human condition of suffering, beyond the relative form. You are literally transformed into being in this world, but not of this world. You experience life to be miraculous. You experience enlightenment and are set free.

The Practice of Meditation

Now let's talk about when and where to meditate. For me, I set up a meditation room in a walk-in closet, where I have a mirror, candles, and spiritual symbols to help me follow my ritual. Deepak Chopra and most of the meditation teachers recommend setting up a specific place in your home, or having a specific place where it becomes your own sacred personal space. Also, the more you can meditate at the same time each day, the easier it will be to develop a habit and a daily spiritual practice. We have found that the more of a ritual it becomes, the more likely you will incorporate it in the long-term. Some people prefer to meditate amid nature and may do different hikes or walks at a different location each time. What is important is that your practice works for you and that it is in alignment with your *Divine* expression. Meditation is for you, so remember to "know thyself and be true to thyself."

Begin with ten minutes in the morning and follow up with ten minutes in the evening to become centered and to silence the mind. You can work up to thirty minutes in the morning and thirty minutes in the evening, or as long as you desire. Sit in a quiet space and begin to silence the mind, taking a few deep breaths and focusing on just *being*. Close your eyes and fall into the void of nothingness. If it helps, focus on your breath, releasing all thoughts. When thoughts start to stream into your mind or when you start having conversations with yourself, simply notice them. Do not try to control them or stop them; just witness them like clouds rolling by. If you drift off, it is ok, just bring your *Consciousness* back to the present. Do not make yourself wrong or judge yourself if you get entangled in a thought. Simply come back to the here and now. Remember that just because a thought comes through, it does not mean you must engage it. Notice the eternal aspect within, beyond thinking.

Detach from identifying with your thoughts. We often get confused and identify ourselves with our thoughts. We think we must feel this way because we thought it. We become reactive to our own thoughts. Instead, you have a choice as to which thoughts you want to keep and which thoughts no longer serve you. Remember that you are not your thoughts, you are the thinker. Exhale and embrace the journey.

Day 34 Practice

MEDITATE

LAW OF GIVING AND RECEIVING

The Universe doesn't know the difference between giving and receiving. They are both divine exchanges of energy; the expression of love. For us to receive we must give and vice versa. The extent to which you give what you desire equals the degree that the Universe will abundantly shower you with what you desire. This interchange is the currency and flow of prosperity.

Today's practice is to **MEDITATE!**

➢ Practice meditating for 10 minutes in the morning and 10 minutes in the evening.

➢ Sit in meditation position with your legs crossed or sit in a chair with your spine erect.

➢ Focus on the inhale and exhale of your breath.

➢ Observe your mind chatter, bringing your focus back to the breath.

➢ If your mind wanders, simply observe and bring it back to the present.

Day 35

Mindfulness: The Eternal Now

"What day is it?" asked Pooh

"It's today," squeaked Piglet. "My favorite day," said Pooh.

~AA Milne

What if I told you that you have the potential to hear the heartbeat of the *Universe*? What if I told you that you could hear the internal guru that has the wisdom of the most intricate intuition within? What if I told you that you could listen to others' souls and their hearts' deepest desires? What if I told you that through your listening from a clear space, you could create miracles in the lives of others? There is something yearning to be heard, something longing to be known, an experience of listening from the heart and soul: listening from the eternal sacred space within. It is from the depths of the ether that permeates and connects everyone and everything. It is a divine echo of utter ecstasy. It is the voice within reflected through space and time.

Have you ever truly listened to anyone? Have you ever truly been listened to? In today's world, we not only have a million things going on in our lives, but we have a billion thoughts going through our minds. We think we are listening, but we are not. In fact, you may consider that you have never truly heard anyone because you have been listening through your own perception, lens, and restricted awareness. Mind chatter blocks your ability to be fully present and filters cloud your reality. You have layers and layers of judgments that narrow your view and strip away all that is available and reachable to you.

To truly listen, you must listen from the eternal aspect of yourself, the part of you that is changeless and all knowing. There are infinite levels of listening; however, the most important is the one between you and your Higher-Self. Once you can hear the depths of your own soul, it is easier to hear the depths of the souls of others. Listening with your whole being can feel miraculous and opens doors to the *Universe* you did not even imagine existed. We all think we listen, but there are so many levels, variations, and depths of listening which we can fine-tune.

The world has a plethora of vibrations and sounds that we often do not hear. I am not talking about the idea that sometimes when talking to other human beings, you miss their point of view or are blind to their *Truth*. If you think about sound and listening in terms of vibrational waves travelling through different mediums to connect you to the *Universe*, it makes sense that your environment affects what your metaphorical and physical ears are tuned to hearing.

Echolocation, which is also referred to as biosonar, is the biological sonar that is used by many animals. Animals send signals out to the environment and can hear the echoes of those calls from the things around them. They locate and identify objects by listening to these echoes. Animals use these as locational guides and for hunting (Jones, 2005). Consider the ways in which you listen to the world around you, how it speaks to you, and what it is communicating from its core. Listening remains one of our greatest tools, a substantial source of connection and an ever-evolving discovery system.

The miracle of listening can only be done in the eternal now. Mindfulness is the ever presence of having awareness to all of life. It is practicing the use of our mind and how that affects the experience of each moment. In our culture, we have been trained to live in our heads, not in our hearts or bodies. Our entire school system is based on the development of our logical thinking and not on our experiential process of evolving and creating. Most people have so much mind chatter that they feel there is an entire circus of monkeys living in their heads at all points in time. We are bona fide walking zombies in a real-life video game, compulsively and meticulously on the defense of life. Meditation is a concept so powerful that Harvard Business School offers a course to build the inner strength of the great minds that are destined to be our next world leaders. But it isn't just a tool for the intellectually elite; this is a revolutionary movement and skill that can profoundly impact anyone's experience.

The primary practice of being mindful is being present. Most of the time, you are either living in the past or the future. When you live in the past, you often encounter regret, shame, remorse, angst, resentment, or a generalized sadness for the loss of someone or something. When you live in the future, you tend to live with anxiety, feeling as if you won't arrive to the destination you desire, and are deeply fearful of the unknown. In the spiritual realm, there is no such concept of time; all things in the past or future that instill negative emotions must be released to be here, in the present, and in the now.

Become the Observer

Just as in meditation, one of the tools to help you stay present is to become the observer and witness your life. This is the eternal presence within that never changes and that has always been present. It is the aspect of yourself that doesn't have judgment and is non-reactive. Again, the moment anything happens in life and you assign it a positive or negative meaning, you instantaneously experience a positive or negative effect within you.

When you stay in neutrality and simply observe whatever is or is not occurring in life, you can begin to consciously choose how you would like to respond instead of reacting. Staying focused allows you to accomplish what you desire and it allows you to fully experience the process, seeing, smelling, and breathing in all the wonderful roses along the journey. You are a director of energy; honing your skills by staying focused is a beautiful discipline that allows you to fully embrace the game of life and human endeavor.

Notice your thoughts as they wonder off to yesterday and tomorrow. Consciously bring your thoughts back to where you are right now. Look to your environment to land you in your senses; smell the fragrance, see the colors, feel the temperature,

REV. DR. ERIN FALL HASKELL

touch your skin. Ground yourself to Mother Earth and feel the energy going through you into the whole *Universe*.

Day 35 Practice

PRACTICE BEING PRESENT

LAW OF HARMONY

There is Divine order to this Universe. To the extent that you create harmony is the extent to which you will experience free will. There is a standard we have created that demands that we must create in harmony to be unbound. The Universe is constantly guiding you towards a harmonious life. Through freedom of choice you can arrange things in such a way as to set in motion a series of causation that will harmonize your own conditions without antagonizing the like power by others.

Today's practice is to **BE PRESENT!**

➤ Practice staying neutral to what does or does not occur today.

➤ Practice observing people's viewpoints, perceptions, and belief systems.

➤ If you do feel reactive today, remember you're not your beliefs, thoughts, or emotions; you are the creator of them.

➤ Practice observing your internal mind chatter, bringing your mind back to being present.

➤ Practice non-judgement and non-attachment today.

REV. DR. ERIN FALL HASKELL

DAY 36

Language: The Power of Your Word

Truth is such a rare thing, it is delightful to tell it.

~Emily Dickinson

Your entire world is created into existence by the words you choose to speak. You were invited in an earlier chapter to open to the possibility and the *Divine* reality that you literally speak your world into existence. Your *Subconscious* and the entire *Universe* is listening to every single word you say and responding with one answer: *Yes!*

The law must respond to what you speak out into the world through *The Law of Correspondence*. Words can break someone's heart or uplift it. They can plant the seed of chaos or harmonize your world through artistic poetry. Words make up the substance of the books we read and the powerful lyrics of the songs that change the world. They can be the creation of the start of war or the declaration of peace. Words can inspire us to do things we never thought possible, and birth modern inventions that help bring everything together. They can be the last straw of an already broken relationship or be the vows of an eternal marriage. Words are powerful.

Logically and energetically, you enter into agreements with others based on how you speak about yourself, how you speak about your life, and how you speak of others. Think about it. Next time you go to lunch with a friend, notice how they speak their world into existence. Do they speak scarcity or abundance? Do they focus on how life is difficult or how life is easy? Do they view people as having limitations or endless possibilities? Do they speak powerfully, placing their dreams into reality in this moment in time or somewhere in the far off never-never-land? Do they speak like a victim or as someone who is the co-creator of life?

If you want to know someone's future, just listen to the things they say. You do not have to go to a fortune-teller or a psychic; you can simply listen to how they are creating their life by listening to their choice of words. Once you become aware of this phenomenon, you often choose to be around people who see others in good light. We've all been around people who talk poorly of others and come to realize that they are most likely doing the same about us as soon as we leave the room. When you realize the power of words, you usually choose to be around people that see everyone for their full potential and *Divinity*.

Integrity

People can be great talkers, but their actions may be less than desired. We call these types of words *empty words* because they do not mean anything. Overtime, they have zero power. Often, you view people that do not live in alignment with their word as people you should not trust. Our culture has taught us to believe that these are immoral people; however, this correlation is simply a cause and effect phenomenon.

When someone tells you that they will do something and they do not, your natural reaction is to stop believing what that person says. It is as simple as that. If you want to be someone whom people view as powerful, then your words must match up to your actions, nothing more, nothing less. Words are the creative substance of the experience of your life; they are the impetus of the circumstances of the life you lead, and they are the link between the ethereal and the physical. They are powerful because you give them power. Use them as the expression of who you desire to be. May your words set you free to live a life you love.

Day 36 Practice

SPEAK YOUR WORLD INTO EXISTENCE

LAW OF TRUTH

At the core of who you are lives an omnipotent presence that has eternal wisdom and love. Within each cell of your body lives a divine intelligence, an innate healer, and an unlimited life force. You are endowed with intuition and universal guidance. The extent to which you deny this is the extent to which you will suffer.

Today's practice is to **SPEAK YOUR WORLD INTO EXISTENCE!**

➢ **Be mindful:** Begin to be conscious of how you are speaking your world into existence. Notice how you speak of others. Notice any limited beliefs you are creating through your words. Notice if you are speaking your dreams into existence powerfully or in a dis-empowering manner (Example: I am trying to write a book or I am writing a book).

➢ **Empty the *Consciousness* of dis-empowering words:** Release all negativity, victim-hood, gossip, manipulation, complaining, scarcity mentality, social dogma, judgments, and problems. Let go of words such as "try," "someday," "maybe," "I can't," etc.

➢ **Create your world powerfully into existence:** Speak with authenticity, creativity, possibility, integrity, and from the heart.

Day 37

Visioning: Unveiling Your Truth

My method is different. I do not rush into actual work. When I get an idea, I start at once building it up in my imagination. I change the construction, make improvements and operate the device in my mind. It is absolutely immaterial to me whether I run my turbine in thought or test it in my shop. I even note if it is out of balance. There is no difference whatever, the results are the same. In this way, I am able to rapidly develop and perfect a conception without touching anything. When I have gone so far as to embody in the invention every possible improvement I can think of and see no fault anywhere, I put into concrete form this final product of my brain. Invariably my device works as I conceived that it should, and the experiment comes out exactly as I planned it. In twenty years, there has not been a single exception. Why should it be otherwise? Engineering, electrical and mechanical, is positive in results. There is scarcely a subject that cannot be mathematically treated and the effects calculated or the results determined beforehand from the available theoretical and practical data. The carrying out into practice of a crude idea as is being generally done is, I hold, nothing but a waste of energy, money and time.

~Nikola Tesla

In 2006, the blockbuster movie *The Secret,* hit televisions and computers around the world. It was based on *The Law of Attraction* and taught people how to get what they wanted through positive thinking. After two episodes on The Oprah Winfrey Show, *vision boards* became the rage in manifesting. People began to cut and paste images from magazines into collages, displaying visions of the lifestyle of their dreams. The problem came when people either were unable to demonstrate what was on their *vision board,* or when manifestations happened, people still felt unfulfilled with the tangible items they had manifested. Critics began to magnify the pitfalls of manifestation; however, many people could still see how it was a great introduction for the world to begin the conversation about how our vibration creates our experiences.

After my *Awakening,* I realized that manifestation without an *Awakening* can lead to a trap. It is like entering a maze hoping to arrive to some destination, but instead, you keep encountering dead ends. Without a true purpose, life can feel empty and feel like it has no point.

Awakening to Your Vision

Visioning is an authentic process of getting in alignment with your true self and in turn, with what your Higher-Self knows you desire. It is living your calling, your *Truth,* and purpose into form. In this process, ask *Spirit* (your Higher-Self) open-ended questions to manifest the unfolding of your *Divine* vision to emerge.

Nikola Tesla, the famous inventor, used *Visioning* to manifest and create his work. He produced over 300 inventions all of which began with an intense visioning process because he truly understood the power of the mind.

Emptying the Consciousness and transformation through visioning is the process of going beyond your present paradigm out-picturing of who you are. Visioning is very different from creating or imagining a vision. Most of us have all created *Vision Boards*, cutting out pictures from magazines and taking the time to imagine them as reality. Unfortunately, one of the biggest lessons one can learn from creating a 'Vision Board' is to be careful what you ask for. Many visions you create are out of ego, only getting you more 'stuff' to manage, and keeping you distracted from the real vision. They merely lead you to acquiring the next material possession, only to realize you are still not fulfilled. Fulfillment and joy come when we are living out our *Divine calling*, aka *Life's Purpose Statement*.

Commit to living your truth and vision by practicing the following, "Each day, I will take the time to go into silence and commune with *Source*. I will ask purposeful questions and hold space for the answers to be heard. I will be a listening vessel for the *Divine*. Then, as I go back into the world, I will ask if I am in alignment with that vision. I will honor my vision."

Day 37 Practice

PRACTICE VISIONING

LAW OF VIBRATION

Life is a constant energy exchange through the communication of frequency. Everything is in motion, nothing is solid, and change is inevitable. The vibration of your life is created by your beliefs and the choices you and the culture make, which create a certain magnetism within your body, mind, and soul through the circumstances of your life. High vibration is in direct correlation to aligning with Universal Laws and Mother Nature.

Today's practice is to **PRACTICE VISIONING!**

Begin Meditation

Do this by finding a quiet space, getting into meditation position (sitting cross-legged), closing your eyes, quieting the mind, and focusing on that which is real (that which is the eternal space beyond anything that is transient in the physical realm). The main purpose of getting into this space for visioning is to become a 'listening vessel' for your *Highest Consciousness* by clearing the mind chatter and becoming as present as possible. Focusing on the breath is a wonderful way to tune oneself to the eternal now.

Ask Questions

Begin to ask questions to your Higher-Self. For example, what is my unique gift to give to the world? What is seeking to emerge in the unfoldment of my calling? What is my unique purpose in this life? What is my individual divine expression in this lifetime?

Remember, there are two types of questions: open-ended or closed. It is important to allow *Source* to answer from an open-ended question when visioning; furthermore, there are two primary types of open-ended questions. One comes from scarcity and fear and the other comes from abundance and prosperity. The *Universe* will answer both, so be conscious of how you are directing it.

Next, think about who you need to become to manifest that vision. Michael Beckwith (2009) has a genius analogy of the concept that anyone can 'get' things through manipulation, but to keep them, you must have the *Consciousness* of it. He gives the example of two men, one has the *Consciousness* of prosperity and the other one does not. One gets a car by stealing it, but to keep the car, he must keep stealing. The man that has the prosperity *Consciousness* owns the car, and when it gets stolen, all he must do is call up his insurance agency and ask for a new one. You cannot have the life you desire until you become the essence of the person that would have that life. You cannot become a professional until you embody the knowledge and live that knowledge.

Ask Deepening Questions

What gifts, talents, and capacities do I already have that I can implement now that can be of service to my vision? How can I serve my vision today? What can I let go of that which no longer serves my vision? Does this habit serve my vision? What thoughts, perceptions, and circumstances do I need to become more conscious of?

These questions are to help advance more understanding around what lessons still need to be learned, what skills need to be developed, what communities to engage with, what people to surround yourself with, and what capacities to advance. This is the work to get out of your own way so that you can step into who you need to be to live your vision.

When you embody your authentic essence, the *Universe* adjusts accordingly, bringing all people, things, and community that are in alignment with that frequency. Form always follows *Consciousness*. This is the *Law of Attraction*.

Feel Your Bliss

As you feel the joy from the fantasy of having your vision come to life within your *Consciousness,* energize and inform your Subconscious with the positive frequency. Feel your bliss by dramatizing the emotions that you would have upon your vision becoming reality. While still in meditation, feel the emotion of motion that draws you to take bold action around your vision.

Imagine yourself living your vision. What does it feel like? What are you doing on a day-to-day basis? Who are you spending time with? Where are you living? How do you spend your mornings and evenings? What sounds do you hear when you envision it? What meals are you tasting? Use your imagination to experience all of your senses. A true vision meditation will compel you to take 'right action' towards manifestation. This is the *Law of Action*.

End with Gratitude & Take Action

End your visioning session with words of gratitude. This will invoke more feelings of joy and solidify the informing of Truth into your *Subconscious* and *Universal Law*.

Once you have your vision, it is important to not tell it to anyone who doesn't believe you are capable of achieving it. It is a sacred contract between you and your Higher-Self. However, your vision is not set in stone, but it is like a horizon that is always directing you and moves and evolves. Let your vision guide you and inspire you to take bold action now!

Day 38

Intuition:
The Knowing Within

Cease trying to work everything out with your minds. It will get you nowhere. Live by intuition and inspiration and let your whole life be Revelation.

~Eileen Caddy

It has been called the sixth sense. It is the intangible, the ethereal, the intelligence distanced from reason and logic, a knowing. It is not anything that can be scientifically proven; yet it can feel more real than the most solid object in this world. So, what is this thing called intuition? Intuition is the spiritual guide within that is like an angel's eye that reveals the unseen. It is the boss, the conductor, the pilot, the grand master; illuminating the grandest path for your journey. When you live from spiritual *Truth*, your logical mind serves in conjunction and with perfect synchronicity of intuition. Intuition no longer is a separate faculty, but an instrument in the grand symphony of your *Divine* song of life.

Intuition is *Spirit*, your *Higher Consciousness*, communicating through a *knowing* that guides and directs you on your path of *Truth*. This gut feeling transpires through the spiritual plane, beyond the bounds of space and time, beyond all reason or linear thinking. It is a natural faculty that serves your highest good; a GPS tracking system built inside of you, only it does not direct you towards a certain position on Earth, but rather, navigates you towards your highest good. It is like a built-in mechanism that navigates and gives off alarms or a *knowing* when you get off track. It can also send flashes of insight, like a *Divine* fortune cookie with pieces of wisdom of the future, and a glimpse into your destiny.

Often, you suppress and deny this profound inner guidance system, denouncing it and consequently disempowering your abilities to use this precious tool. If honed, it can often be the best faculty for making those tough decisions in life. Intuition can be strengthened through recognition of it; honoring it and building a feedback system with it. You already know that the *Law of Attraction* dictates that what you focus on, you attract accordingly. If mastered, your intuition can be your greatest strength and ally. Even though it is immeasurable, I put it to you; it is more real than all the tangible material facts of your life.

For most of my life, my intuition would speak to me, but I would not listen. Whether it was a decision I was making about work, an event I was planning on attending, or a relationship I was in, regardless of how my intuition was trying to guide me, I would not listen. My intuition would often tell me which way to go and I would often do the opposite. Today, my eyes are wide open from that eternal inner space and I view and experience intuition completely differently. In fact, I can hardly differentiate intuition from any other aspect of my life because I live in such a transparent authentic way that everything is driven by my spiritual *Truth*. My inner 'knowing' has grown so pure; I listen to my intuition and let it guide me through life. Now I live from *Spirit* instead of emotionally reacting to life.

Today, all aspects of my life are aligned with what my heart and soul desire. Today, I do not listen to my mind chatter or the linear realm, rather, from my gut-knowing and from the spiritual plane. Ernest Holmes said, "These channels represent spiritual capacities since each is an avenue leading to self-knowingness, and self-knowingness is the very nature and essence of *Spirit*."

Day 38 Practice

DEVELOP YOUR INTUITION

LAW OF INTENTION

This law states that what you focus on and give attention to expands, and what you don't focus on or give attention to diminishes. You are a director of this Universal Law; the moment you give energy to any thought it sets life into motion. You are being guided to stop giving energy to things you do not want and begin giving your energy to the things you do want. The Universe is guiding you to go within, get clarity on your authentic desires, and set your intentions every day.

Today's practice is to **DEVELOP YOUR INTUITION!**

Trust Your Gut

Within each of you is a built in navigational system that is constantly guiding you to stay true to yourself and your own personal *Truth*. This is your intuition. There is something you can feel the moment you meet someone, if that person speaks to your heart or not. There is something that knows if the event you are going to attend is in alignment with the passions of your life. There is something in you that knows if you are wasting your time or headed toward your highest vision. This knowing is the internal compass, the captain of your ship, your *Spirit*, guiding you home to your destiny. This does not mean that you make uninformed decisions when making choices within your business or planning the legalities of your life. Building trust within you is part of the journey of living your *Truth*. Trust your gut, be true to yourself, and your intuition will build exponentially.

Trust Your First Instincts

There is an intelligence within you that has the wisdom of the entire *Universe*. Often, your first instinct is that part of you that has not tapped into the limited logical aspect of your mind. Notice instances when your first instinct was correct and acknowledge it so that you can build trust with it.

Keep a Journal

The more you can confirm and acknowledge your intuition, the more you can further develop your intuition. Write down your gut feelings, your first instincts, and your inner knowing. Reflect on your journal entries and contemplate them during meditations.

Meditate Daily

When you quiet your mind, you tap into your Higher-Self, universal intelligence, and *Source*. This is a wonderful place to ask your Higher-Self for answers to questions you have. It is also a wonderful place to ask for guidance. When you move more and more into the eternal space within, you are better able to tap into that space in your normal day to day life. Then you can stay in your intuitive state all of the time.

Day 39

Affirmative Prayer and Affirmations

Treatment is the art, the act, and the science of consciously inducing thought within Universal Subjectivity, for demonstrating that we are surrounded by a Creative Medium which responds to us through a Law of Correspondence. In its simpler meaning, treatment is the time, process, and method necessary to the changing of our thought.

~ Ernest Holmes

As a little girl, I remember being very sad that my mother and father had gotten a divorce. They split before I could even remember when I was just two years old. One day, after seeing a movie where a little girl was praying, I decided to do the same. I went into my room, kneeled on the side of my bed, and placed my hands together in prayer position. I said, "God, please make my mommy and daddy get back together!"

It never happened. So, from that point on I decided that God must not exist or something must be wrong with me that would impede God from answering my prayer.

Most people believe that prayer is asking for something; a new circumstance to arrive, a material object to show up, a relationship to enter their life, a better body, a raise in pay, etc. Prayer is portrayed to be something you do when you are helpless, sad, and desperate. Often, it is perceived as something only done by religious people who revere a prophet, entity, or something greater than themselves.

It wasn't until my mid-twenties that I began to understand what prayer was from a metaphysical perspective. Never truly believing God was some man in the sky, I looked to the place where science and spirituality met, New Thought Affirmative Prayer.

PRAYER IS THE MOVEMENT OF ENERGY UPON UNIVERSAL LAW FOR A SPECIFIC DEMONSTRATION

Prayer is the expanding of *Consciousness*, unleashing the infinite innovation within and setting the polarity of *Universal Law* into motion. It is the recognition that there is One Omnipotent Energy that has, and is, creating the entire *Universe*. As you unify and identify as that same Life Force, you experience your true *Spiritual Powers*. In the revealing of this *Truth*, you release limiting beliefs and direct energy upon *Universal Mind* for a definite result. Energizing the pictures within the mind with gratitude enhances your intentional manifestation. Furthermore, releasing the attachment and control of the outcome allows for perfect unfoldment.

What is it?

Affirmative Prayer is one of the primary tools to direct your thinking and energy upon the *One Mind* with a specific purpose, which in turn, informs *Universal Law,* instantaneously transforming your world and your experience of it. It is an active Creative Process within the individual. Treatments are intended for specific outcomes which all include expanding your *Consciousness*, releasing limited beliefs, *Awakening* the infinite innovator within, and revealing the *Truth* of who you are. All of which shifts your magnetic field and energetic frequency, changing your relationship to all of life.

How Does It Work?

The vibration of the feelings within your thoughts is what directs the *Universe*. When you are going through the five steps below, it is important to remember that *feelings* are what inform *Universal Law.* Your intention that back your words create the feelings and the vibration that you send out to the *Universe*. You could do a 'Spiritual Mind Treatment' without saying anything if you direct your mind and feel the elation from the thoughts that you create. In treatment, the perception of the self, shifts, and therefore, all of life shifts. As Thomas Troward states, "this is the triumph of principle over precedent, of the working out of an idea to its logical conclusions despite the accumulated testimony of all past experience to the contrary."

Spiritual Mind Treatment can be incorporated into any *Consciousness* work, anytime you are not feeling empowered, when your feelings are negative, or if you simply want to direct energy, raise your vibration, and improve the quality of your thoughts. It can be used to reveal the *Truth* about illness, relationship issues, career or money situations, emotional states, or any circumstance on your mind. Personally, I love to begin my day with a treatment to invoke my highest conscious state to be the most present and productive every day. It can be used to help keep your thinking in alignment with your spiritual principles; ridding your life of limited beliefs, complaining, victim mentality, fear, gossiping, scarcity mentality, and all that keeps you from living your full potential.

Two Types of Affirmative Prayer

Argumentative: This is where you use spiritual logic to argue for the *Truth*. In this type of treatment, you acknowledge the unwanted circumstance of your life and you actively make the case for the absolute spiritual *Truth*. For example: If you were experiencing a lack of money, you would make the case for the *Truth* of the *Universe*, which is that there is only abundance and that you claim it now. This type of treatment is not as frequently used because it tends to interfere with focusing and directing energy upon *Universal Law*. The Steps of Argumentative Prayer include: (a) recognition, (b) unification, (c) realization, (d) condition, (e) realization, (f) gratitude, and (g) release.

Realization: This is where you reveal the *Truth* within your *Consciousness*. In this type of treatment, you completely turn away from the circumstance and focus on the spiritual *Truth*. For

REV. DR. ERIN FALL HASKELL

example, if you are experiencing lack of money, you would not think of the situation, rather you would focus on the five steps of Realization treatment as follows: (a) recognition, (b) unification, (c) realization, (d) gratitude, and (e) release.

How to Do It?

Before taking the steps of Spiritual Mind Treatment, it is best to set your intention to the exact thing you are treating. State the condition you would like to explore and in which circumstances of your life you are ready to reclaim your power. What are you ready to heal? Who are you ready to become? What limitations are you ready to let go of? Within treatment, you do not treat for the circumstances of someone's life, but of the mindset and freedom of choice. Demonstration is the effect of the mind. Although many miracles take place instantaneously within treatment, this is not the focus.

Let's pretend the person doing this treatment is feeling a little down and confused about the direction of her life in the realm of her career and purpose. She would state, "The intention of this Spiritual Mind Treatment is to expand my *Consciousness* and gain clarity around my purpose and calling within my career."

Step One: Recognition & Acknowledgement. This step acknowledges that *Awakening* is from *One Source* that has created all of life. It is this *One Life Force, One Infinite Creative Substance*, which resides within and as everything. You recognize that the first cause is *Spirit*, which is *Consciousness*. In this phase, you acknowledge eternity as both the finite and infinite, the microcosm and the macrocosm. In recognizing this *Divine* intelligence as the first and only cause of all of life, you begin to open your *Consciousness* to the unbounded *Truth*. The first principle of Spiritual Mind Treatment is understanding that you are surrounded by an infinite intelligence.

Example: In this sacred moment, focusing on the breath of inhaling and exhaling, I notice the point where they come together. In this state of presence, I experience where the finite transcends into the infinite. I recognize that there is no breath without a body to breathe; there is no oxygen to breathe without the trees that have been nourished by the sun, rain, and Mother Earth. I acknowledge that this life force touches all, interconnects every one of us to the entire *Universe.* This life force nourishes every cell of my body. It is the spark of every thought. It is this same *Divine* source that holds the stars in the sky and turns the night to day. It is that which connects all of life through the body, mind and *Spirit,* transcending the life cycle of your humanness into your eternality. I recognize that there is only *Consciousness,* this *One Life Force* that has created every last drop of this *Universe.*

Step Two: Unification & Oneness. Having recognized the magnificence and awesome power of the *ONE* presence that is absolutely everything, unify this same intelligence as your own *Consciousness*. Within this step is the unification of your individual mind to your Universal mind, merging into your highest *Consciousness*. You *Awaken* and become aware of your Divine Nature and ability to co-create with all of life. This is the revealing of spiritual inclusivity and understanding that there is no such thing as duality. No such thing as a separate thing called evil. All of life is one grand organism of *Consciousness*.

Example: As I step into the *Consciousness* of *Oneness,* I realize that I am *One* with the All. I am that. Within me is the highest *Consciousness* that is the same creative substance that has created mountains and the greatest inventions of our ancestors. There is no division, there is only *Divine*. I unify myself from the individual *Consciousness* to the highest *Consciousness* by simply allowing the *Truth* to be known. I am aware of my *Divine* nature and the *Truth* of my spiritual nature.

Step Three: Revealing & Healing. In this step, you direct energy upon the Cause-and-Effect *Universal Law* for a specific outcome. With the frequency and vibration of your word, you declare and command the Creative Medium. You summon and set the *Intelligence* into motion knowing that it corresponds and reflects your beliefs as the circumstances of your life. This is done through the conviction of your thought and the feelings that back your words. This is where you reveal the *Truth* about the circumstances of your life. This is where the healing takes place through the revealing of the *Truth* of who you are. Again, you do not treat for conditions to change; you treat for healing within the mind that has caused the circumstances. You reveal the spiritual *Truth*. In this step, you act as the masterful conductor of this specific Grand Symphonic Song through your word.

Example: I declare that within me is total clarity because the soul is never neutral. I know that within me is a passion so great, that it is the gift I am to give the world. It is myself in its highest expression. I know that within my *Subconscious* mind is the bubbling forth of this purpose. I command that *Truth* come forth now. In speaking my word, I inform the subjective mind and set *Universal Mind* into action. There is only clarity and joy at the heart of my being.

Step Four: Gratitude & Thanksgiving. In this step, you shift your attitude into gratitude, transcending the thing itself further into action. It is through gratitude that you open your *Consciousness* to receiving good. This state of mind is the highest vibration of energetic flow. Within this joyous state, you imagine and know wholeheartedly that whatever has been desired, directed, and demanded, has already been created in *Consciousness*, and is being delivered now through the universal medium of the *Law of Correlation*. The only conscious work to do is to bask in the receiving and elation of the prayer being answered.

Example: And so, I energize this *Truth* with the vibration of my feelings of gratitude. I am so thankful for this purpose and clarity. I am so grateful for this revealing. Within my *Consciousness*, I see it and feel it now. I bask in the mental answer that has been revealed. I receive my purpose and calling. I receive my joy and bliss.

Step Five: Release & Let Go. In this step, you let go of all thoughts of outlining and controlling of "how" the perfection of this spiritual mind treatment unfolds. This is the Conscious handing over of your life to your Highest-Self. This is the declaration and commitment to live in faith and act out of *Divine* inspiration. This is the art of allowing.

Example: Now, I release my word to *Universal Law* knowing that my word is the law and has set into action the correlation. I let go and step into grace. I know the perfection of the unfoldment and allow my highest *Consciousness* to flow. It is done!

Affirmations: Mantras of Intention

Affirmations are statements based on truth and intention. They reprogram the *Conscious* and *Subconscious Mind* to align with what you are committed to embodying. Affirmations should be stated multiple times throughout the day. The more repetitive you say your affirmations, the more your beliefs will shift. My suggestion is to pick one and repeat it as many times as possible as you go through your day. You can even record yourself saying the affirmation and listen to it in your car, while you work out, or even when your sleep.

So, how do you know which affirmation you should use? First, notice what negative talk you tell yourself and begin to flip it into an affirmation. Example: If you keep telling yourself that you are not enough, flip it into an affirmation.

Negative Talk: I am not enough
Affirmation: I am more than enough, I am a divine spiritual being worthy of every dream I can imagine!
Negative Talk: I will never get a decent job

Affirmation: The *Universe* is abundant and I claim my perfect job!

Negative Talk: Life is hard

Affirmation: Life is a divine adventure; I choose to love all of it!

Negative Talk: I have low energy and feel helpless

Affirmation: I live powerfully with passion and purpose!

Day 39 Practice

PRACTICE AFFIRMATIVE PRAYER & AFFIRMATIONS

LAW OF NATURE

There is a Divine source and intelligence inherent in all of life. It establishes and regulates the phenomenon of how elemental forms of matter relate. This law dictates the chemistry, biology, and science of the mechanics of this world. This natural design brings structure and standardization to create in a context of organization.

Take some time today to **PRACTICE AFFIRMATIVE PRAYER & AFFIRMATIONS!**

➤ Pick an area of your life where you feel dis-empowered and practice an affirmative prayer.

➤ Set the intention of your prayer before beginning.

➤ Treat until you experience an epiphany around the area of your life you are treating for, until you feel a new sense of 'knowing', or until you demonstrate what you were treating for.

➤ Shift a negative belief you have into an affirmation and repetitively state it throughout the day, energizing it with positive feelings.

Day 40

40-Day Practices

Ask yourself whether the dream of heaven and greatness should be waiting for us in our graves or whether it should be ours here and now on this earth.

~Ayn Rand

The moment you begin your *Awakening*, the lens you've been looking through at life shatters and you have to take off the foggy glasses you once wore. Your eyes squint at first, adjusting to the light that blinds your eyes.

You stand there, realizing life isn't what you thought it was; it isn't a place to tend to your comfort or a fairy tale movie. It can feel meaningless and trivial. There may even be a point of not wanting to live.

You enter a standing room where hope and desire don't reside, nor peace and serenity. It is like a treasure hunt, where you go searching and seeking, but figure out the secret to exiting is counterintuitive, and you have to surrender.

You begin *Awakening* to the holographic *Universe*, where every morsel of your identity shape shifts the cosmos, and where radars no longer track the speed of cars, but the speed of thought.

You begin *Awakening* to the fact that every relationship is the invitation to experience the depths of your B.S. (Belief Systems) and entanglement that furthers your human vicious cycle or a gateway to a quantum leap spaceship.

You abandon your pity party; the blame, shame, and guilt game, no longer fulfilling your appetite for misery. Someday, victimhood, perfectionism, and judgment become lies you're not willing to tell yourself anymore. No more shoulds or coulds, expectations, or needing validations. You've suffered long enough.

You begin *Awakening* to the profound and poignant etiquette of only sending good vibrations through the ether, knowing the boomerang effect of life can knock you flat on your ass if you don't respect the *Laws of the Universe*.

Packing your bags, you join the Spiritual Hitchhikers and head to the infinite journey within. Like diving deep in the ocean, you must come up for breath. With spit and mucus, you inhale like your life depends on it.

But over time, the more you submerge, the more the reality in the physical world seems unreal. Like a dream that begins heavenly, turns to hell, and eventually reverts back to paradise. The more you take the plunge into the depths of your soul, into the ethereal realm, the more you experience freedom.

Your heart beats a little stronger, you no longer react to the outer world, you breathe with a knowing, and you love yourself a hell of a lot more.

You begin *Awakening* to the *Truth* that you're not here to win the rat race of materialism, but to experience the depths of your soul in form. You're here to produce the greatest product, YOU! You are Awake!

40-Day Practices

To stay in the heavenly realm, I've found that having a Daily Spiritual Practice along with doing 40-Day Practices is the best combo to support this endeavor. In experiencing a wide variety of spiritual practices, modalities and processes, one of the most profound impacts on my life has been engaging in 21, 30, and 40-Day Practices. Both current science and biblical teachings back the belief that creating habits through repetition is one of the most profound ways of transforming one's life. There comes a time in your Spiritual Journey where you have reached a point called *input overload*. You have read almost every book on spirituality. You have gone to enough seminars, spiritual retreats, cleanses, and meditations to know that you still aren't walking your walk. It is one thing to 'talk the talk' and it is another to 'walk the walk.' It's time for your *Awakening* and to live your *Truth!*

Committing to your spiritual practice is integrating your discipline to overcome negative thinking and actions. It is one major key to unlocking your chains of suffering. New actions create neurons and form new habits so that you can live in alignment with your *Truth*.

So, how long does it take to create a new habit? According to Dr. Maxwell Maltz (1960), the famous surgeon who noticed how long it took for his patients to get used to seeing themselves after an amputation, found that it is at least 21 days. In his best-selling book, *Psycho-Cybernetics,* he showed examples of how amputees stopped feeling phantom sensations after 21 days. He claimed that engrams, which are memory traces, produce neuron connection and neuro-pathways that can be changed after 21 days. Other spiritual leaders and great writers point to the 40-day mark to be 'Reborn.' Phillippa Lally (2009) conducted a study in which she found that it took anywhere from 18 to 254 days. Based on multiple research studies, it appears it can take between two to eight months, thus having a 40-Day practice gets you in the practice of creating long-term habits.

Pick something that you feel would better your life and develop skills you love. You will be expressing and living life more fully. If you have always wanted to be a dancer, then dance for the next 40-days. That could consist of dance classes, going out dancing, dancing at home to videos. If you have always wanted to write a book, then write every day, blog, or journal. If you have always wanted to be healthy, then exercise for an hour every day. You could choose different types of exercise each day. One day you might just walk for an hour, the next you might go to the gym, the next you might go for a hike, etc. If you want more money, you might spend time everyday focusing on getting new clients or a new job. If you want to stop being lonely or bored, commit to getting out and being social for 40-days straight by going to lunches, meet-ups, and social gatherings.

The talented artists of this world did not wake up one day and become the best in their craft. Every day they did what they loved and over time they grew their skills to extraordinary perfection of self-expression. One day at a time, turns into months, turns into years, turns into a lifetime. Let's face it, we are habitual beings. Let's create the habit of doing things we love.

The best way to be consistent is to make yourself accountable. One way of doing this is with a friend so that each of you communicates daily when you have fulfilled that day's commitment. This can turn into a fun activity with a simple text that states 'Day 1 of 40 days complete!'

You may have a commitment that inspires you regarding the physical aspect of your life. There are unlimited 40-Day Practices of the body. You could take on detoxing and cleansing for the duration of the time, or take on a simpler task, such as walking for 20 minutes a day. The point is that whatever you choose to do, do it for the 40-days. Do it every day without skipping one day. This not only builds new habits, but builds confidence and restored integrity and trust within yourself. We speak volumes to ourselves through what we are committed to do. Who are you committed to being when it comes to the wellness of your body?

Choose one thing to commit to every day for 40-days and remember to state it in the positive instead of the negative (Examples: Instead of saying, "no sugar for 40-days," say, "whole foods that support my blood sugar levels for 40-days." Instead of saying, "no complaining for 40-days," say "creative and grateful words for 40-days").

Day 40 Practice

PRACTICE, PRACTICE, PRACTICE

LAW OF INDIVIDUALIZATION

You are the individualization of the One Spirit, a unique Divine expression. It is your specific use of the One Mind. Universal Laws are designed to be uniquely directed by each person for specific experiential outcomes. Furthermore, you are the only person in the entire Universe with your Divine gift, YOU!

Today's practice is to take on your next 40-DAY PRACTICE and **PRACTICE, PRACTICE, PRACTICE**!

Here are a few examples:
- ❖ Affirmations three times a day
- ❖ Meditate for 20 minutes a day
- ❖ Whole foods for 40 days
- ❖ Write one blog post each day
- ❖ Learn something new every day
- ❖ Walk for 60 minutes a day
- ❖ Write a letter of gratitude to someone new each day
- ❖ Do something you've never done before each day
- ❖ Write a new song or poem each day
- ❖ Network with three new people each day
- ❖ Perform a random act of kindness each day
- ❖ Journal about intuition each day

References

ACS (n.d.). Discovery and development of penicillin. Retrieved from https://www.acs.org/content/acs/en/education/whatischemistry/landmarks/flemingpenicillin.html

Adams, S. (2012). Why winning powerball won't make you happy. Retrieved from http://www.forbes.com/sites/susanadams/2012/11/28/why-winning-powerball-wont-make-you-happy/#618cdc9c6e3a

American Foundation for The Blind (n.d.). Helen Keller biography. Retrieved from http://www.afb.org/info/about-us/helen-keller/biography-and-chronology/biography/1235

Associates Mind (n.d.). Allegory of the long spoons. Retrieved from http://associatesmind.com/2013/11/19/allegory-of-the-long-spoons/

Backster, C. (1968). In evidence of a primary perception in plant life. Retrieved from http://www.rebprotocol.net/clevebaxter/Evidence%20of%20a%20Primary%20Perception%20In%20Plant%20Life%2023pp.pdf

Baars, B.J. (2007). The global workspace theory of consciousness. In Velmans, M. & Schneider, S. (eds.), *The blackwell companion to consciousness.* Malden, MA: Blackwell Publishing.

Beckwith, M (2009). True abundanceawa Practices for living from the overflow on CD ROM. [CD ROM]. Louisville, CO: Sounds True, Incorporated

Borelli, L. (2014). Brain on sex: How the brain functions during an orgasm. Retrieved from http://www.medicaldaily.com/brain-sex-how-brain-functions-during-orgasm-274052

Boyd, D. (2013). The voice of serendipity. *Psychology Today*. Retrieved from https://www.psychologytoday.com/blog/inside-the-box/201305/the-voice-serendipity

Campbell, J (2014). *The hero's journey: Joseph Campbell on his life and work.* San Francisco, CA: New World Library.

Choi, C. (2011). Building blocks of DNA found in meteorites from space. Retrieved from http://www.space.com/12569-meteorites-dna-building-blocks-discovery.html

Chopra.D. (1993).*Creating affluence.* San Rafael, CA: Amber-Allen Publishing.

Corliss, J. (2014). Mindfulness meditation may ease anxiety, and mental stress. *Harvard Health Publications*. Retrieved from http://www.health.harvard.edu/blog/mindfulness-meditation-may-ease-anxiety-mental-stress-201401086967

Descartes, R. (1637). Discourse on the method of rightly conducting the reason, and seeking truth in the sciences. Retrieved from https://www.marxists.org/reference/subject/philosophy/works/fr/descarte.htm

Einstein, A. (1954). *Science and religion.* New York, NY: Crown Publishers.

Emoto, M. (2010). What is the photograph of frozen crystals. Retrieved from http://masaru-emoto.net/english/water-crystal.html

Erhard, W. (2013). Werner Erhard quotes. Retrieved from https://wernererhardquotes.wordpress.com/tag/love/

Frankl, V. (2006). *Man's search for meaning.* Boston, MA: Beacon Press.

Harvard Health Publications (n.d.). Understanding the stress response. *Harvard Health.* Retrieved from http://www.health.harvard.edu/staying-healthy/understanding-the-stress-response

Haskell, A., personal communication, June 8, 2016

Hay, Louis (1984). *You can heal your life.* Carlsbad, CA: Hayhouse, Inc.

Hippocrates (n.d.). Encyclopedia.com. Retrieved from http://www.encyclopedia.com/people/medicine/medicine-biographies/hippocrates

Hirshberg, C., & O'Regan, B. (1993). Spontaneous remission bibliography project. Retrieved from http://noetic.org/research/projects/spontaneous -remission

James, S.D. (2009). Female orgasms may be tied to rule of thumb. Retrieved from http://abcnews.go.com/Health/ReproductiveHealth/sex-study-female-orgasm-eludes-majority-women/story?id=8485289

Jones, G. (2005). Echolocation. *Current Biology* 15(13), 484-488. Retrieved from http://www.cell.com/current-biology/abstract/S0960-9822(05)00686-

X?_returnURL=http%3A%2F%2Flinkinghub.elsevier.com%2Fretr
ieve%2Fpii%2FS096098220500686X%3Fshowall%3Dtrue

Jowett, B. (2005). *Essential dialogues of Plato*. New York, NY:
Barnes and Nobles.

Lally, P (2009). How are habits formed: Modeling habit
formation in the real world. *European Journal of Social
Psychology*. Retrieved from
http://onlinelibrary.wiley.com/doi/10.1002/ejsp.674/abstract

Lama, D. (2005). *The universe in a single atom: The convergence
of science and spirituality*. New York, NY: Morgan Bond Books.

Lipton, B. (2015). *The biology of belief*. Carlsbad, CA: Hayhouse
Inc.

Maltz, M (1960). *Psycho-Cybernetics*. New York, NY: Simon &
Schuster.

Manocha, R. (2001). Researching meditation. Clinical
applications in health care. *Diversity Natural and
Complementary Health*, 2, 2-10.

Mastin, L. (2010). The human memory. *Neurons and Synapses*.
Retrieved from http://www.human-
memory.net/brain_neurons.html

McGreevey. S. (2012). Imaging finds different forms of
meditation may affect brain structure. *Harvard Gazette*.
Retrieved from
http://news.harvard.edu/gazette/story/2012/11/meditations-
positive-residual-effects/

Moore, A. (2009). Relocating Marie Bonapart's clitoris.
Retrieved from

http://www.academia.edu/192016/Relocating_Marie_Bonapar te_s_Clitoris

Ogden, D., Carroll, M., Kit, B., et al. (2012). Prevalence of childhood and adult obesity in the United States, 2011-2012. Retrieved from http://jamanetwork.com/journals/jama/fullarticle/1832542

Oizumi, M., Albantakis, L., & Tononi, G. (2014). From the phenomenology to the mechanisms of consciousness: Integrated information theory. Retrieved from http://dx.doi.org/10.1371/journal.pcbi.1003588

Perry, T. (1978). In tree roots: Facts and fallacies. Retrieved from http://arnoldia.arboretum.harvard.edu/pdf/articles/7884.pdf

President's Cancer Panel (n.d.). The president's cancer panel. Retrieved from https://prescancerpanel.cancer.gov/#front

The Tech (2013). How do genes work. Retrieved from http://genetics.thetech.org/about-genetics/how-do-genes-work

Pressfield, S (2012). *The war of art: Break through the blocks and win your inner creative battles.* New York, NY: Black Irish Entertainment.

Psychologist World (n.d.). Stress, flight or fight response. Retrieved from https://www.psychologistworld.com/stress/fightflight.php

Ray P. & Anderson S., (2001). The cultural creatives: How 50 million people are changing the world. New York, NY: Broadway Books.

Schwatz, B. (2009). The paradox of choice. Why less is more. New York, NY: Harper Collins.

Science News (1998). Quantum theory demonstrated. *Observation Affects Reality.* Retrieved from https://www.sciencedaily.com/releases/1998/02/98022705501 3.htm

Seifer, M. (2001). Wizard: The life and times of Nikola Tesla: Biography of a genius. Pasadena, CA: Book Alley.

Seppala, E. (2015). How meditation benefits CEO's. *Harvard Business Review.* Retrieved from https://hbr.org/2015/12/how-meditation-benefits-ceos

Serendipity (1989*).* In *Oxford English dictionary online* (2nd ed.). Retrieved from http://www.oup.com

Shuttleworth, M. (2009). Hawthorne effect. Retrieved from https://explorable.com/hawthorne-effect

Simmons, D. (2008). Epigenetic influences and disease. Retrieved from http://www.nature.com/scitable/topicpage/Epigenetic-Influences-and-Disease-

Smythies, J.R., Edelstein, L., & Ramachandran, V. (Eds.). (2014). The claustrum: Structural, functional, and clinical neuroscience. Amsterdam: Academic Press.

Solar Plexus (2001). The oxford companion to the body. Retrieved from Encyclopedia.com: http://www.encyclopedia.com/medicine/encyclopedias-almanacs-transcripts-and-maps/solar-plexus

Talbott, S (2007). The cortisol connection. Alameda, CA: Hunter House.

The Energy Project (2016). We are energy champions. Retrieved from https://theenergyproject.com/about

Tiller, W.A. & Dibble, W.E. (2009). White papers: A brief introduction to intention. Retrieved from http://www.tillerinstitute.com/white_paper.html

Troward, T. (2008). The creative process in the individual. Charleston, SC: Bibliolife.

Truth (1989). In *Oxford English dictionary online* (2nd ed.)., Retrieved from http://www.oup.com

Waterfield, R.H. (Ed.). (1990). Conversations of Socrates. London, NY: Penquin Classics.

Weil, A. (2016). Stress and anxiety. Retrieved from http://www.drweil.com/health-wellness/body-mind-spirit/stress-anxiety/dealing-with-stress/

Wolf, F.A. (n.d.). Fred Allen Wolf, Retrieved from http://www.fredalanwolf.com/#AK

Wolfe, D. (2016). Harvard MRI study shows meditation rebuilds brain's grey matter in 8 weeks. Retrieved from https://www.davidwolfe.com/meditation-rebuilds-brains-gray-matter-in-8-weeks/

Zemblanity (n.d.). Zemblanity. *World Wide Words*. Retrieved from http://www.worldwidewords.org/weirdwords/ww-ser1.htm

ABOUT THE AUTHOR

"There are moments in life when something happens, life alters, and your entire perception transforms instantaneously." For Erin, that *Awakening* moment was 22 years ago when she was holding her stillborn son in her arms, just after giving birth to him. "Tears were streaming down my face as I looked at his beautiful body and realized his body was still there, but he wasn't. I realized he wasn't his body; he is a spiritual being. One can conceptually understand that we are not these bodies, but I got it on an entirely different level. My entire world crumbled, delivering me to spiritual revelation." This sent me on an intense spiritual quest traveling around the world, discovering truths, and learning how to live and embody the truths that had been revealed.

Erin lives in Los Angeles, where she is a Doctor of Divinity, TV Host, New Thought Minister, Mother, Best-Selling Author, Keynote Speaker, and a lover of life. She also hosts the Dr. Erin Podcast and holds Mastermind Leadership Programs for thought leaders. Her mission is *Awakening* a billion people globally to their *Divinity* and life's purpose, and assisting them in manifesting their dreams. She teaches people how to reprogram their *Subconscious*, align with their personal *Truth* and *Universal Law*s, and create their daily spiritual practice. She mentors people one-on-one on a body, mind, and spiritual level. She believes that when someone *Awakens*, they naturally have a gift and message to bring to the world.

After many years of working with a wide range of clients; from top celebrities to single mothers, she wanted to bring her programs to the world. She believes that the route to happiness and fulfillment is not just knowing the *Truth*, but living the *Truth*!

In the Light,
Dr. Erin

FREE GIFTS & MENTORSHIP

FREE 30 GUIDED MEDITATIONS
www.DrErin.TV
www.ErinFallHaskell.com

FREE SUBCONSCIOUS MASTERCLASS
With Purchase of Book
www.ErinFallHaskell.com/AwakeningBook

30-DAY PROSPERITY
Claim Your Birthright of Abundance!
www.30DayProsperity.com

THE DIVINE MASTERMIND
12-Weeks to unleash your life's purpose, reprogram your *Subconscious*, and manifest your dreams! Are you tired of going around in circles, never able to manifest your dreams? Are you tired of feeling overwhelmed, confused, and having to do it all by yourself? Are you losing your confidence? In this program, you will learn step-by-step how to create your life's purpose statement, how to create masterminds in the four areas of your life, and learn how to reprogram your *Subconscious* mind. Breakthrough your limiting beliefs that are sabotaging your success and create a life you love. There's only one thing standing between you and your dreams: procrastination. It is time to become the thought leader you were born to be and bring your message to the world. www.TheDivineMastermind.com

ONE-ON-ONE MENTORSHIP
➢ Spiritual Entrepreneurship
➢ Mind Subconscious Work
➢ Body Cleansing and Detoxing
www.ErinFallHaskell.com

BOOKINGS & SPEAKING
erin@erinfallhaskell.com

Made in the USA
Lexington, KY
15 May 2019